Experiencing

CHRIST

In Communion

52 Devotionals for the Lord's Supper

Experiencing

CHRIST

In Communion

---

52 Devotionals for the Lord's Supper

By
Gary Cottrell

MDC Press
Lexington, SC

ISBN 13: 978-0615790930
ISBN 10: 0615790933

Cover design by Derek Chiodo
http://www.ecovermakers.com/

To the members of the Northwest Church of Christ, St. Petersburg, Florida, and the Lexington Church of Christ, Lexington, South Carolina, for all the ways they have provided encouragement and support.

Acknowledgments

I would like to express my gratitude to Karyl Burress, Fran O'Dell, and Sandy Barnett for reviewing the manuscript and making numerous suggestions for improving it. The book is better for their input.

Special thanks must also go to the elders and members at the Northwest Church of Christ in St. Petersburg, Florida, as well as those at the Lexington Church of Christ in Lexington, South Carolina. Both of these congregations allowed me the freedom to expand my own experience at directing the congregation before experiencing the Lord's Supper. They consistently put up with my experiments without a word of criticism, when some of my attempts did not quite work out as well as I had hoped. More importantly, they encouraged me, both in the presentations I made and in the preparation of this book.

Table of Contents

How You May Use This Book

Because these devotionals are specifically designed for congregational use, there are fewer restrictions than one would normally find in a published work. At the same time, this book is copyrighted, and there are limitations on the use you may make of it. For this reason, I wish to say a few words about what is allowed and what is not allowed.

What Is Permitted

Because these devotionals are intended to be used, not simply read, you are being granted more freedom than might normally be allowed. Here are some examples of what you are **permitted** to do.

• A congregation may purchase a copy of this book to make available to its members. A congregation **may not** make photocopies of this book to give or sell to its members.

• You may read any of these devotionals directly from the book without acknowledging the source. You may make a photocopy of a devotional for this purpose if you choose.

• You may take these devotionals and write your own outline for presentation.

• You may rewrite these devotionals to suit your specific beliefs or your congregation's needs. In some instances I have suggested ways in which you might effectively make them more personal.

• You may use these devotionals in a class or instructional setting, to help others learn how to be more effective in their own presentations. For instructional purposes you are allowed to provide the class with photocopies of up to two of these devotionals. If you use any portion of this book in an instructional setting, you are required to acknowledge the source, just as you would for any other book.

• In some instances the lessons may suggest an idea you want to develop in your own way. This also is permissible.

What Is Not Permitted

While you are being given a great deal of latitude in your use of this book, there are some restrictions. Here are some examples of what you **may not** do.

• You may not photocopy this book in its entirety, either for your own use, or to give to someone else.

• You may not distribute either this book or any part of it in print or electronic form for someone else.

• While you are not required to cite this book if you are presenting a devotional to a congregation, you are not allowed to claim any portion as your own work.

• You are not permitted to publish any of these devotionals or ideas derived from them in any form.

In summary, you may not do anything that affects either the identity of the author or the financial impact of this book.

You may not do anything which would eliminate the need for yourself or someone else from buying a copy of this book. So, while a congregation may make a copy available to its members in the church library, no individual is allowed to make a copy available to another person, although you may lend a copy to someone. The determining factor is that only one person will be able to use a copy at the same time, and no copies from a single copy may be made for others to use.

Please recognize that these devotionals reflect the fruit of many years in which I have had the privilege of presiding at the Lord's Supper. They also represent hundreds of hours of writing, rewriting, proofreading, and editing. As such, you are expected to abide by the copyright restrictions that come with any published work. Feel free to take advantage of the great latitude being allowed, but also respect the effort that is represented by this book.

Introduction

The Lord's Supper — the Eucharist — the Mass — Communion. Different Christian groups use many words to describe what has, from the earliest period of the church, been considered one of the primary expressions of our faith. In the tradition in which I was raised, we most often refer to it as the Lord's Supper or Communion, two words which emphasize both its connection with Christ, as well as our relationship with Him and with one another.

Whatever term you use to describe it, virtually every Christian group recognizes the importance of this practice. Throughout the centuries, Christians have also understood that the significance of the Lord's Supper goes far beyond its use as a symbol. It has always been understood to embody a powerful means of reminding Christians of the importance of words such as Atonement and Resurrection, concepts that, at our best, we have difficulty comprehending.

Churches are increasingly coming to recognize the value of providing a devotional before the Lord's Supper to help members focus on the significance this portion of our service should have for each of us as we partake of it. Unfortunately, too often congregations give little or no training to those who perform this most important function, and the result is predictable. Depending on the individual, any number of problems can turn what should be an inspiring focus on our Lord into a distraction. This book was written as an aid to those whose function it is to help the congregation benefit from their participation in the Lord's Supper. For many years, it has been my privilege to preside at the Lord's Supper. Over the years, I have observed every mistake it is possible to make (and committed most of them myself). At the same time, I have been truly inspired by others who have skillfully used this time to focus our attention on the living Christ. I offer a few suggestions to help you as you prepare for this most important function.

How to Make an Effective Presentation

If we truly believe that the Lord's Supper is important, surely we should desire to do everything possible to make it a meaningful experience for those participating. The elements required to achieve this are not especially difficult, but they can determine whether the experience inspires or actually detracts from what we are trying to accomplish. Consider carefully the suggestions given. They can make a real difference in how your congregation experiences the Lord's Supper.

Don't Inform — Inspire

The Lord's Supper was never intended to become a dry ritual or an intellectual exercise. It should be a time when we feel, as well as remember, the power of the gospel message. Virtually everyone who takes the Lord's Supper will already know the basic facts surrounding Jesus's sacrifice for us, and they do not need to be instructed about that. Your purpose should be to help the congregation feel the significance of His death, burial, and resurrection.

Obviously, there are times when you need to present facts, but do not stop with mere information. Take those facts, and help your audience appreciate their significance. This book provides many examples of how to accomplish this. Just one example is in the lesson titled "I Remember." The devotional starts off by asking the congregation to consider what might have happened in later years if any of Jesus's apostles ever got together and took the Lord's Supper. It includes instances taken from scripture that provide examples of incidents the apostles may have remembered later in life.

But the lesson does not end there. The devotional goes on to consider how we too have experiences with the living Christ which should inspire us. It reads:

> Memories! So many memories! But how does all that relate to you and me? We weren't there that night. We can read about it in the gospels, but how can we too remember?
>
> The only way we can also remember is if we too have had experiences with the living Christ.
>
> "I remember how He rescued me from the life I was living before. I can't comprehend what my life would be if it had not been for His forgiving love."
>
> "I remember when tragedy seemed to overwhelm my life, and grief and depression were more than I could bear alone."
>
> "I remember when another Christian said such harsh and uncaring things about me, when I was struggling to do God's will the best way I knew how."
>
> "I remember how through it all, He has always been there to carry me, when I could not carry myself."

And then we close with the haunting last line. "I

remember . . . I remember."

Do you see how this approach does so much more than simply telling your congregation about what Jesus's death accomplished? It provides an emotional appeal that should make all of us feel the love of Christ as we take the Lord's Supper. Give this kind of powerful message, and your presentation will be more likely to succeed in doing what you want it to do.

Keep It Short

The most common mistake made by those who preside is making their comments too long. I have sat in services in which the person presiding spoke for over twenty minutes. This results in the pulpit minister having to make a painful choice. He must either shorten his own sermon, to which he has given hours of preparation and prayer, or have the length of the service go way over what the members have prepared for.

Lincoln's "Gettysburg Address" demonstrates how effective this principle can be. His speech was only two minutes long, but it was so powerful this short message honored the fallen and helped solidify support for the war. In doing so, Lincoln's speech has become a part of literary history.

Shortening your remarks does not mean sacrificing quality. In fact, more often than not, just the opposite is true. Blaise Pascal is said to have written a letter in which he said, "I'm sorry I wrote you such a long letter; I didn't have time to write a short one." While that may sound strange, it is often true. Long and wordy presentations are often the result of a lack of focus and preparation. I am convinced that devotionals at the Lord's Supper should rarely (if ever) last more than five minutes. In reality, some of the most inspiring I have ever heard were only one or two minutes, because the speaker had prepared the presentation well and was focused on achieving the desired effect. Congregations will remember three or four minutes of a presentation as they take the Lord's Supper. If the message is much longer than that, they will tend to become distracted and lose focus. Often when the devotional is too long, it is because the one speaking has tried to do too much. You are not there to preach a sermon. Remember, the purpose of the devotional is to help the congregation focus on the significance of the Lord's Supper. There should be only one point to your presentation, and it should be clear and direct.

Make It Real

People feel differently about using illustrations. Some see them as tools to help the congregation identify with the comments; others prefer using only Biblical texts or stories. Both have value, and in this book you will find examples of both approaches, so you may choose what you prefer. That being said, there are both pitfalls and benefits that can come from using illustrations. Be aware of both.

Remember that the Lord's Supper should normally be a time of reflection. A number of the devotionals included in this book came from my own experiences. While I encourage you to seek examples and illustrations from your own life, you need to be careful. What may seem funny and memorable as we describe our children's antics may appear irreverent to others.

At the same time, illustrations from our own lives are appropriate, and they are certainly Biblical. Jesus often used parables to help His listeners understand what He was teaching. But the stories should be directly related to the point you are trying to make. They should also be appropriate in both tone and content to the purpose of focusing the congregation on the Lord.

The devotional titled "D-Day" is intended to be a modern parable that uses an example from history with which most of your audience can identify. At the same time, with the appropriate music, the story vividly tells the story of how Jesus took upon Himself the battle we could not win, and because of His death, gave us the victory over sin and death. The illustration delivers a relevant message, is appropriate in tone, and provides a powerful emotional experience that helps the congregation focus on Jesus. That is what you are trying to achieve.

Illustrations must be appropriate, and they need to be incorporated into your presentation with care and skill. But when used properly, they can become a powerful tool that transforms the Lord's Supper from something we do out of habit into a living connection to our everyday lives. Above all, never lose sight of the purpose of the Lord's Supper. Certainly, it should serve as a reminder of the death of Jesus. At the same time, we should do everything possible to keep the Lord's Supper from becoming a dry ritual that fails to stir our hearts. Properly used, illustrations can make the Lord's Supper real to Christians in the twenty-first century, just as Jesus's parables made His teaching relevant in the first century. Make the Lord's Supper real for the congregation. If you do that, you will have succeeded.

Humor

The Lord's Supper is normally a time of reflection, usually focusing on the death of Christ. For this reason, humor is very rarely appropriate. Indeed, until you become experienced at presenting devotionals for the Lord's Supper, it would be best to avoid humor completely. Within certain limitations, however, even humor can be included effectively, although it must be used to serve a serious purpose and employed with great care.

Perhaps the most effective use of humor in this collection is in "Easter." Look at how this devotional begins.

The story is told about a little girl who was really getting excited just before Easter. She couldn't help thinking about the Easter bunny, the candy, the eggs, and all that goes with the holiday.

Her mother, recognizing that this just might be a teachable moment, took the opportunity to tell her about Jesus, how He died and was buried, but that He didn't stay dead, but rose again and is alive today. The little girl beamed and asked excitedly, "Oh, then will Jesus be at church this Sunday?"

"Will Jesus be at church this Sunday?" That's an interesting question, isn't it? Do we really believe that Jesus is here today?

The humor is apparent, and we expect the congregation to laugh. Then, after a meaningful pause, the speaker repeats the little girl's question followed by the serious observation, "That's an interesting question, isn't it? Do we really believe that Jesus is here today?" The combination of the humor immediately followed by the sobering question, changes the tone as we consider the reality that Jesus is with us, not just on Easter Sunday, but every day of our lives. In this instance the humor actually reinforces the seriousness of our faith that Jesus really is with us. By doing so, the humor even intensifies the significance of the power of the resurrection and its reality for our lives.

Use humor cautiously and only when it helps achieve a clear purpose. Do not dwell on the humor. Make the application quickly and move on. Ask yourself whether the point is made better with humor. If you are uncertain, leave it out of your presentation.

Organize Your Thoughts

Nothing can take the place of adequate preparation. Since

your message is short, you should take the time to write it out, even if you are planning on presenting it from memory or using an outline. If it is too long to write out, it is too long — period! You need to shorten it.

Remember your audience. You will find that the devotionals included here are written in a colloquial form of English. For instance, contractions are used frequently, because more than likely, that is the way we will normally present the devotional. Remember, you are not delivering an academic paper. You are trying to help your congregation identify with the lesson you are presenting. There is certainly a place for formal writing, but I would suggest that your devotionals will have more meaning if presented in an informal speaking style.

Practice Your Presentation — Aloud

It is absolutely essential that the one presiding take the time to practice the presentation aloud, just as it will be presented to the congregation. I would suggest that you practice it at least five or six times. If you are self-conscious, go into your bedroom and close the door. Practicing aloud allows you to know just how long your presentation will be. If you read the devotionals in this book exactly as written, they should never exceed five minutes; however, if you prepare your own comments (which I encourage you to do) or even an outline of one of these devotionals, you may be surprised how long the presentation can become.

Practicing aloud several times also provides an

opportunity for you to present your ideas with a polish that can only come with repetition. Verbal preparation allows you to express your thoughts without stumbling. You can also be more effective by emphasizing words or phrases, or by a pause at just the appropriate point to emphasize what you are trying to say. Please do not neglect this final, but important part of your preparation.

Some may object that this is theatrical and has no place at the Lord's Supper, but every good speaker (including, I suspect, your preacher), uses these techniques. Most people would never consider doing any public speaking without thoughtful preparation. Does not preparing people to commune with our Lord deserve equal attention?

Final Thoughts

The Lord's Supper must never become simply a ritual or an intellectual exercise. When we preside at the Lord's Supper, we are not seeking to provide information. Our purpose is to help the congregation feel the significance of what they are about to do and to focus on the Lord. The devotionals in this book are written with this goal in mind. All of them are short. The illustrations have been selected with the belief that they are appropriate to both the subject and the solemnity of the occasion. Most of all, these short talks are designed to assist you in focusing your congregation on our Lord and His sacrifice for us. They are offered with the hope that they will help you make the

Lord's Supper the central part of your worship, just as we try to make Him the Lord of our lives.

New Beginnings

The New Year is typically a time for making resolutions, more often than not, resolutions that we really know we're not likely to keep. At the same time, I'm sure that many of you can attest that new beginnings can work, and they don't always come at the beginning of the year.

Many of us have experienced the difficulties that come with moving to a new city. The obstacles can be daunting. Just getting around without getting lost is hard enough. And making new friends can also be challenging. While a new church can be exciting, it may be hard (and perhaps embarrassing at first) trying to match names with faces.

At the same time, the process of moving can provide an opportunity to start over without the baggage, both literal and figurative, that we might want to leave behind. We aren't bound by the preconceptions of the people who knew us before. The opportunities for spiritual growth are certainly available, as I suspect many of us have experienced.

The Lord's Supper celebrates the most significant new beginning in history, because it reminds us that Jesus provided us with that new beginning by taking upon Himself all that old baggage that each one of us cannot get rid of on our own. And He goes further than that. Yes, Jesus has taken upon Himself all of our sins, thus allowing us to start fresh. Even more, God also fills us with His Holy Spirit, providing us with the strength to make that new beginning work.

Because of what Jesus did on the cross, we can have a

new beginning anytime we want to claim it. So today we celebrate both Jesus's death, and also our new life.

Death Row

Finally they were coming for him. Oh, it had taken sixteen years. After all, he had a good attorney who knew how to work the system. He had filed appeal after appeal, each time pretending that this would be the one to set him free. But in his heart the man knew that all they were doing was buying time.

You see, he was guilty. How often he had tried to rationalize. "You don't understand; it was him or me. That's the way things work in my world. What good was he anyway? The world's better off without him. I did society a favor."

The man had said it so often that at times he almost believed it. But there were other times. On death row you have time. What a paradox. You have time, but you know that really time is the one thing that is so limited. And at night, in the dark and the quiet, the man saw clearly what he had done, and he knew there was no real excuse. So his life would end like this. A lethal injection, a moment of dementia, then what? Now he would find out.

Somehow he found the strength to walk down that bleak hallway without having to be supported. "Put on a brave front. Give the papers at least one good thing to say. 'He knew how to die well.'" Before the man even realized it, he was strapped to the gurney. The warden had read the death sentence and walked away. Now he waited.

Suddenly he heard a disturbance outside. The warden burst into the room and gave him the incredible news. "You're free. I don't understand the details, but your sentence has been vacated. In the eyes of the law, you have been declared completely innocent. You can walk out right now."

As the puzzled man was led from the death chamber, he passed a room where another man lay dead. An older woman (probably his mother) sat crying next to the body. And in some manner that he could not have explained, the man sensed that this man and he were linked in some way.

A fanciful story certainly. It doesn't really make sense, because, you see, the truth doesn't make sense. But it's still the truth. In 1 Corinthians 1:18, Paul recognizes this paradox when he says, "For the message of the cross is foolishness to those who are perishing, but to us who are being saved it is the power of God."

You and I were on death row. *Perhaps some of you still are.* And in our hearts we recognize that we deserve our fate. But we fight it anyway, even though we know we'll lose the battle in the end. And then what?

Here then is the truth. We were all under sentence of death; not just physical death, but spiritual death — eternal death. And we were guilty. But the Father sent His Son who took upon Himself our guilt and our punishment. We can say it in a multitude of ways, but in the end that's what Christianity comes down to. It doesn't make sense; it sounds totally fanciful. But it just happens to be true.

Today we take the Lord's Supper to remember that one fanciful, illogical, but powerful truth. Jesus took your place on death row, and because of Him, you can walk out of your prison — pure, and clean, and free. That's what we celebrate when we take the Lord's Supper.

Wash One Another's Feet

Read John 13:1-5

Most of us are probably familiar with this story. In the following verses we read of Peter's response and Jesus's mild rebuke of him. Peter was embarrassed at the violation of etiquette that Jesus had made by doing a job that was normally reserved for a slave; never realizing that in just a few hours Jesus would demonstrate the ultimate example of servanthood by going through the agony and death of the cross.

I wonder how often we're concerned with what we feel are the important things, while ignoring the problems staring us in the face. Are we so disturbed about the direction our society is taking that we've become oblivious to the needs of our neighbor? The reality is that our neighbor may be the key to fixing the issues in our society. There's little I can do to resolve the overall problems in this country. Oh, I can write the president and my congressman, and perhaps I should do that. But I'm becoming more and more convinced that the only way we can truly make this a Christian nation is by converting our neighbor to Christ. And the most authentic way of doing that is simply by presenting the gospel message after our neighbor has come to respect us as people who truly care about them and who live out our faith in our lives.

In verses 12-17 of John 13, Jesus explains why He washed the disciples' feet. It was to give them an example, so that they — that is, "we" — should wash one another's feet. For Jesus that meant a cross; for us it will most certainly require sacrifice of some sort.

Today we remember the sacrifice that Jesus made for us. Yet let us not forget that, while we can never do what He did, we have our role to play. Sacrifice is woven into the very fabric of our Christian faith, and just as Jesus took up His cross, so in some manner must we.

Recognizing Value

Suggestion — You might begin with a specific example. I began this presentation by holding up a tiny piece of coal for which I had paid $25.00. I then went on to explain how this coal was salvaged from the wreck of the Titanic and was worth the price to me. Perhaps you have a rare coin, an old newspaper or other document. A visual example of something for which someone paid more than it would normally be worth helps make your point more effectively than simply saying the words.

Read Matthew 13:45-46

How do we determine the value of something? Some people are willing to pay quite a lot for an item that's practically worthless to others. That's the whole idea behind garage sales. We've all heard the expression, "One person's junk is another person's treasure." A coin can be worth thousands of dollars, a painting by Picasso, millions. You see, value really is determined by what someone is willing to pay.

What is your own worth? I suspect far too many of us don't have a high enough sense of our own value. If it's true that the value of something is determined by what someone is willing to pay, consider the price God paid for you. He was willing to allow His Son to be tortured to death in the hope that you might respond to that love. Doesn't that sound like He considers you of great value?

We should not be surprised if the world doesn't

understand the value each of us has in the sight of God. In a sense, I still do not understand why He considers me worth it, but as we take the Lord's Supper, we are confronted again with the undeniable reality of His love for us. We don't have to understand that love; all we need to do is accept it. And if we do, the power of that love can begin to transform our lives.

As you take the Lord's Supper, remember that the only One who counts believes that you are valuable indeed, and He showed it by dying on a cross.

When Everything Changes

Think back on a time in your life when everything changed. You don't have to live very long before that happens. Significant change can come in so many forms. Some of them are good. You married the girl or guy of your dreams. You got a job or promotion that you were hoping for. A child was born, and you knew your life would never be the same again.

But not all change brings happiness. That beautiful marriage can become plagued by bitter conflict or even end in divorce. Instead of getting that job you wanted, you might lose the one you have, and with it your self-esteem, followed by fear of what the future may hold. That child, for whom you would gladly give your life, may develop a serious illness, be born with a disability, or choose to go down paths that break your heart. Almost all of us have experienced events that changed our lives forever, and I suspect as I've been talking, specific images formed in your minds.

We live in a culture that seems to be searching desperately for a better life, but at the same time refuses to embrace the changes that could make that better life possible. The television show, *Intervention*, describes real-life situations in which people with addictions are confronted with the reality of their destructive behavior and are also offered the resources to turn their lives around. One amazing aspect of virtually every episode is that invariably the person living with the addiction fights desperately against any offer of help. They appear to be afraid of what a new life without the addiction might look like.

In the 1970s there was a poster that was centered on the Lord's Supper. It pictured a loaf of bread and a cup of wine. But it was the caption that spoke volumes about what the Lord's Supper represents. It read, "To believe in God is to believe that tomorrow can be different from today."

And despite the denial, isn't that the message a lost world so wants to believe? We know it's true, because we can see the desperate search, even if in all the wrong places. We seek fulfillment in so many things. Some are clearly destructive — drugs, alcohol, gambling. Still others seek meaning in dark pleasures — sex or pornography. Others look for more acceptable outlets — job, money, fame.

But none of these avenues can really fulfill our deepest needs. John tells us why in 1 John 2:17. "The world and its desires pass away."

If we really want our life to count for something, it has to be for something eternal. And that's the hope that Jesus offers us. The Lord's Supper reminds us that, when it came down to it, Jesus did not see Himself defined by the pleasures of this life. You may say, "Sure, it was easy for Him. He knew what lay ahead." Yes, that's true. Jesus may have had an advantage you and I can't comprehend. But does it make sense to reject the lesson, just because Jesus saw further than we do? Why not instead decide to accept His understanding, not just of eternity, but His vision for us and what we can be?

To the historian, the Last Supper was about death, but for us it truly is about life; Jesus's resurrection, certainly, but also our life. And it can happen in a moment. Today, right now, your life can change forever. All you have to do is imagine that it's possible. "To believe in God is to believe that tomorrow can be different from today."

Valentine's Day

For some of us the words "ritual" and "tradition" have come to have negative connotations. Perhaps we've experienced what can happen when rituals become dissociated from the truths they are meant to reinforce, and traditions take on the force of binding authority. Certainly rituals and traditions can be abused, but they also have the power to add richness and meaning to our lives as well.

We celebrate Valentine's Day every year and in pretty much the same way. In our culture the ritual has come to center around giving our loved one flowers and/or candy. As I said, we do this every year. The holiday embodies both a ritual and tradition. But, husbands, can you imagine what the response might be if you were to tell your wife that Valentine's Day is just a meaningless tradition and that we should just skip it this year? I would not suggest we take that approach. Why is this ritual, this tradition, important? Because it reinforces in our wife's heart and mind that we do love her and value her. Just as she wants to be reassured, so we also need to be reminded of those qualities that made us love her in the first place.

The Lord's Supper is a ritual, but at this point the analogy breaks down, because God doesn't need to be reminded of our love. But there is more to the analogy. Just as an earthly father delights in his children's expressions of love, perhaps it's not too much to believe that God also delights in our affirmations of love. That in itself is an indication of just how great His love is.

It's still true that we need to be reminded of all those things He has done that brought us to Him in the first place. And the most significant act was, of course, Jesus's death on the cross. So today we remember so much more than the mere fact of Jesus's sacrifice. If we truly participate, we respond again to the magnitude of His love for us, expressed in so many ways we cannot even begin to count them. Yes, the Lord's Supper reflects a tradition; yes, it embodies a ritual. And if we view it that way, it will be nothing more. However, if we choose, we can also experience the Lord's Supper as a powerful affirmation of both God's love for us, as well as our love for Him. Then it is both a ritual and a tradition in the best possible sense.

The Weight of the Cross

Read Luke 9:23-24

Every ten years the city of Oberammergau in Germany hosts the Passion Play, recreating the death of Christ. A story is told about one year when some tourists had come to see the play. One of them asked the actor who portrayed Jesus if he could lift the cross for a moment. Expecting a stage prop, the man was surprised to discover the cross was so heavy he had difficulty lifting it. He asked the actor why he didn't have them make a cross that was easier to carry. The actor responded, "If I could not feel the weight of the cross, I could not play the part."

Although we cannot physically carry Jesus's cross, we can get some idea of how much He dreaded that cross. We see it at the Last Supper. We hear his pleas for release from it in Gethsemane. Perhaps, if we are willing to think about it, we get a glimpse when Jesus staggers and falls under the weight of that cross.

In the passage we just read from Luke 9, Jesus tells us that we too have a cross to bear and that we are expected to carry it daily. What does that mean? Well, for at least one of the disciples, it meant a literal cross. For all of them, with the possible exception of John, it meant dying for Him. When Jesus told His disciples they must take up their own cross, He meant it.

Thankfully, we in America are not threatened with giving our lives for our faith. But let us not dare trivialize what Jesus expects of us. Just what are we willing to sacrifice for Jesus — our security — our job — our home — our stuff? At what point, do we say to Jesus, "Stop, enough"?

But all of that is negative, and I believe the message Jesus is giving is a positive one. "For whoever wants to save their life will lose it, but whoever loses their life for me will save it." (Luke 9:24). That's the real promise. But it's a paradox. Don't all of us know people who, by society's standards, have it all, but who are unhappy, miserable, and lonely? Yet throughout the centuries, those who have been willing to give up everything for Jesus, including their lives, can testify that, even in this world, they have a peace that our society as a whole doesn't comprehend. We can only imagine what they will have in the next.

In one sense Jesus took up His cross, so that we would not have to, taking upon Himself the punishment we should have suffered. At the same time, He has told us that we too have a cross to carry. Let us never forget that.

God Gives the Best

Read Leviticus 22:21-22

God has always demanded the best — a perfect animal, the first fruits. While we may speculate about the reasons for this, at least part of the answer must surely have to do with the absolute perfection of God. He is perfect, and everything associated with Him must also be perfect.

Of course this presents problems for us, for the best we can offer is far from the perfection that would be worthy of standing before a holy God. How then should we respond to that reality? Many people simply ignore or deny their own sinfulness. "I'm as good as the next person." Yes, and as bad as the next person too. And the results are everywhere around us — broken homes, loveless marriages, a desperate search for happiness that this world can never supply. At the same time, far too many people give in to despair and a crushing sense of guilt. For these people life can become a frightening, dark experience, without meaning, and ultimately devoid of hope.

Yet the very characteristic of God that causes Him to require the best, means that He also gives the best. All of those sacrifices that had to perfect — perfect animal, perfect ritual, perfect setting — were but symbols of the one truly perfect sacrifice, when God Himself would offer His very best, His one and only Son. And in that one magnificent, liberating sacrifice, Jesus takes upon Himself all those failures that make me so less than

31

perfect, and He gives back to me His perfection, so that now I can truly stand before God, as Paul said it, "not having a righteousness of my own that comes from the law, but that which is through faith in Christ." (Philippians 3:9).

We complete the circle when we respond in loving appreciation for Jesus's wondrous sacrifice for us. Only then can we become living sacrifices, offering our transformed selves in service to Him. No, we are still far from perfect, but we live in the awareness of two marvelous realities; the continuing ability of Jesus's blood to take away our every sin and the transforming power of His Holy Spirit to help us to become living sacrifices, who will ultimately be able to stand before Him who demands perfection. All of this we celebrate today.

Is Anything Real?

Suggestion — You might wish to alter or add to the beginning a specific example. For instance, when I presented this to my local congregation, I gave a real example in which our family had been in a restaurant which had hot pepper sauce that had Texas in the name, but was actually distributed from North Carolina. That is a slightly humorous way to make the point. Use your own illustration. The possible examples are endless.

We live in a society that seems more and more to be dominated by imitations. What appears to be wooden furniture often turns out to be plywood covered by a thin veneer of real wood. Look at the labels in the grocery store, and you see it everywhere. Fruit juices may have fruit far down in the list of ingredients, if at all. The words "artificial flavor and color" are commonplace.

We see the same thing in other areas of our lives. We have become so accustomed to hypocrisy and deception that, if we're not careful, we can become jaded and cynical. We aren't even surprised anymore when political figures, celebrities, or even religious leaders are revealed to have engaged in multiple affairs. When we hear pending legislation discussed on the news, the accounts vary so widely that we are left wondering if either side is telling us the truth.

Is anything real anymore? Can we believe in anything? What about the story of Jesus? Did that really happen or, as some scholars would have us believe, was the Jesus that lived and walked on the earth radically different from the Jesus portrayed in the Bible?

That's really a complex question that cannot be adequately answered in a couple of minutes today. But let me leave you with one fact to consider. Whatever happened to Jesus, His immediate apostles believed in Him so much they were willing to die horrible deaths, rather than renounce the faith they had. These men, who had been with Jesus, touched Him, talked with Him, listened to Him teach, all said with one voice, "He is the real thing. He is what He claimed to be — the Son of God."

When we take the Lord's Supper, we affirm our conviction, not only that Jesus lived, but that He still lives, and that, because of Him, we too will live forever. We remember His death, but only so that we can say with Thomas, "My Lord and my God!" (John 20:28). Is Jesus real? If He isn't, then nothing is real. But because Jesus is real, you and I are also real, and we have the promise that we will be with Him forever.

I Remember

Read 1 Corinthians 11:24-25

I wonder if in later years any of the apostles ever had the opportunity to sit down at the Lord's Supper together. What thoughts must have gone through their minds? What would they have said to one another? More than anything else, I suspect the Lord's Supper would cause them to remember.

"Peter, do you remember how you promised that even if everyone else deserted the Master, you would never deny Him?"

"John, do you remember how He almost casually announced that someone would betray him? We were all so amazed, we each began to say, 'Surely not I, Lord?' We never suspected Judas, because we all knew the doubts and fears in our own hearts. How blind we were!"

"Thomas, do you remember afterwards when you said you wouldn't believe until you saw Him for yourself? And He showed you, didn't He?"

Memories! So many memories! But how does all that relate to you and me? We weren't there that night. We can read about it in the gospels, but how can we too remember?

The only way we can also remember is if we too have had experiences with the living Christ.

"I remember how He rescued me from the life I was living before. I can't comprehend what my life would be if it had not been for His forgiving love."

35

"I remember when tragedy seemed to overwhelm my life, and grief and depression were more than I could bear alone."

"I remember when another Christian said such harsh and uncaring things about me, when I was struggling to do God's will the best way I knew how."

"I remember how through it all, He has always been there to carry me, when I could not carry myself."

"I remember . . . I remember."

The Reality of Sacrifice

Read the following two passages.
Leviticus 5:6
Matthew 27:35

What most surprises me about both of these passages is their stark simplicity. We commonly read them without pausing to consider what the reality must have been. Josephus tells us that during one Passover in Jerusalem in the first century a quarter of a million lambs were sacrificed. Can you imagine what the temple must have been like — the sights, the sounds, the smells?

Over the centuries, the priests became skilled at killing the lambs quickly with relatively little pain. A crucifixion, on the other hand, was an entirely different matter. The Mel Gibson movie, *The Passion of the Christ*, generated a great deal of controversy when it was released. Whether or not you believe this movie dwelt too much on Jesus's suffering, there is no denying that it was fairly accurate in its portrayal. Crucifixion was no quick knife to the throat, but a slow, agonizing death, preceded by unendurable pain.

And when we pause to consider that Jesus did not have to experience it, we should be even more humbled. How often we have heard that the cross shows us the depth of God's love, and truly it does. How else are we to fathom a love so vast — the God of the universe, through His Son, loves us enough to die — like that!

Maybe the gospel writers didn't like to think about the

37

reality either, and that's why they say almost nothing about the details of Jesus's crucifixion. They didn't need to be reminded of the horror. At the same time, it is comforting to consider that we have a God who loves us enough to die a horrible death for us, and perhaps make us want to love Him just a little more.

Palm Sunday

Read Matthew 21:8-9

This day is generally celebrated in the Christian world as Palm Sunday. The passage we just read gives Matthew's description of what is commonly referred to as "The Triumphal Entry." It describes the last time Jesus went to Jerusalem, exactly one week before His resurrection. Despite the sobering reality that in a few days He would encounter jeers and cursing, on this day Jesus was received as the King He truly was, at least by some of the people.

I can envision at least three groups being present at Jesus's Triumphal Entry. There were His disciples, the Jewish leaders, and perhaps a group of ordinary people. Let's consider for a moment what occurred as far as these three groups was concerned.

First of all, what was their motivation? All the evidence suggests that the disciples still did not understand what was happening. They must have been frightened and confused. The Jewish leaders were suspicious, angry, and judgmental. In Luke's version they said to Jesus, "Teacher, rebuke your disciples!" (Luke 19:39). In other words, "Tone it down, Jesus!" The common people may have heard about Jesus, particularly His miracles. Maybe they wanted a show.

So what did these people do? The disciples walked with Jesus, following Him, because so far it was relatively easy to do so. The Jewish leaders watched and made plans to kill Him. The common people, for the most part, shouted support for Jesus. In John's account the branches are identified as palm branches, from which we derive the name "Palm Sunday." Matthew says they shouted, "Hosanna to the Son of David."

But what happened the following Friday? The disciples were, for the most part, scattered. Only John accompanied Jesus to the end. The Jewish leaders felt they had won. Jesus had been crucified as they wanted. The common people were pretty much the same, curious onlookers. Were any of those who earlier shouted, "Hosanna" among those who later shouted, "Crucify him"? We don't know.

The question though is what about us? Would we have been in any of these groups, and what would our response have been? Hopefully, I would not have been among those who plotted Jesus's death. But what would my response have been? Would I have run away, letting fear destroy faith? Would my "hosanna" have become "crucify him," because each of those seemed to be the popular response on those two separate occasions? Or, like John, would I have stayed with Jesus, even to a cross? As we take the Lord's Supper today, ask yourself the question, "What would I have done about Jesus?" We face that question every day. What was your answer last week? More importantly, what will be your answer this week?

Easter

The story is told about a little girl who was really getting excited just before Easter. She couldn't help thinking about the Easter bunny, the candy, the eggs, and all that goes with the holiday.

Her mother, recognizing that this just might be a teachable moment, took the opportunity to tell her about Jesus, how He died and was buried, but that He didn't stay dead, but rose again and is alive today. The little girl beamed and asked excitedly, "Oh, then will Jesus be at church this Sunday?"

"Will Jesus be at church this Sunday?" That's an interesting question, isn't it? Do we really believe that Jesus is here today?

I would suggest to you that He is with us in at least two ways. He is present in His body assembled here, in each one of us. And His Spirit is also present, because He has promised us that He would be. And so what we are doing is a communion, a communion with one another certainly, but also a communion with our Lord, whose very sacrifice we remember, especially on Easter morning.

I believe, however, the promise goes much further than that. Yes, Jesus has told us He will be with us when we meet together, but the reality of the resurrection doesn't stop there. Jesus has also promised to be with us in all places and at all times. His continual presence should be the motivating power of our lives.

And so, we can rely on that promise when we most need it. Jesus is with us on Monday morning when the stress and pressure of work or school bears down on us. He is with us in the evening when we need his wisdom to meet the crises and difficulties that arise in our families. Jesus is with us when we must say goodbye to the one person who means more to us than anyone else in this world. And it is the resurrected Christ who will be with us when our time also comes to leave it.

Have you had an encounter with Jesus lately? Yes, He is with you today. But remember, He is also with you tomorrow and for all the tomorrows to come. Easter isn't just today. The promise of Easter is for all the days of our lives, and we can still rely on His promise.

"And surely I am with you always, to the very end of the age." (Matthew 28:20b)

When We Don't Get What We Want

Does this sound familiar? You're in a store shopping, and you hear a child asking for something they want. Now, if the child is with a grandparent, they are more likely to get what they're asking for, but if they're with a parent, it may be a different story. If the initial answer is, "No," the child may ratchet up the volume, and often with a scream, yell out, "I WANT IT!" Of course, a little crying never hurts.

Actually, we all know what it's like not to get something we really want. And that experience doesn't go away as we get older; the stakes just get higher. For the child, it may be a candy bar or a cookie. We aren't so childish. What we want could be a new car or a promotion. Tragically, what we fail to get may be even more significant — parents who will love me instead of abusing me, a husband or wife who cares about my needs as much as their own. Yes, we all know what it's like to be denied something we really want.

Did you know the same thing happened to Jesus? Just think back to Gethsemane and listen to the agony with which Jesus begged, "'*Abba*, Father,' he said, 'everything is possible for you. Take this cup from me. Yet not what I will, but what you will.'" (Mark 14:36). Jesus was just like you and me. The cross and everything that went with it terrified Him just as much as it would us. In fact, He was so frightened that He asked His Father for a way out — any way out.

At the same time, Jesus understood that the only way He could get what He so desperately wanted would be to give up on His mission, to renounce the very reason He came to earth. And if He had done that, you and I would be without hope today. We keep seeing Jesus's actions as the measure of His love for us, but I still don't think we truly understand the depth of what He endured for us. Maybe we don't really want to understand.

This much we know. Every child has to come to recognize that sometimes we don't get what we want. The same is true for each of us. Life is filled with choices and conflicts. It isn't getting everything I want. Sometimes it means giving up something I really want, because I want something else even more. I think that's what Jesus ultimately decided. He had to give up something He desperately wanted — to be spared the agony of the cross. But He knew there was something He wanted even more, and that something was you and me. We remember and honor that choice today.

Christianity is Different

Being a Christian does not mean that we must believe that there is nothing good in other religions. While I'm certainly no expert on world religions, it seems to me that all of the largest religions being practiced today include a great deal of teaching about morality and virtue with which we would all agree. If human beings practiced these teachings, it would make this world a better place in which to live.

There is, however, one characteristic which defines Christianity that sets it apart from most other religions in a fundamental way. Most, if not all, of the world's religions demand that human beings achieve perfection by their own strength and will. Different religions use different methods of doing that, whether through performance of specific rituals, living a life of poverty and self-sacrifice, even a belief in reincarnation.

Christians are called to that same goal, but are given a radically different method for achieving it. The Christian belief, contained within the heart of the gospel message itself, is that we are powerless to achieve perfection on our own. Indeed, contrary to what our society is telling us, the message of the gospel is not that we are all good, and that God calls us to accept one another. The message of the gospel is that we are hopelessly entangled in sin and are powerless to get out of it. And because we cannot help ourselves, God, through the sacrifice of Christ, has given us a means of achieving that which all the major religions of the world call us to, not by our own efforts, but by the sacrifice of Jesus who took our sins upon Himself, killed the old sinful nature, and replaced it with His Holy Spirit living within us.

We remember that sacrifice today with both sorrow and gratitude — sorrow that it was necessary — and gratitude that Jesus was willing to endure it for us.

Making It Too Complicated

Suggestion — In the first two paragraphs I describe an incident in my life when I made a situation more complicated than it needed to be. Change those paragraphs in a way that reflects something in your life. It will be a lot more personal and have greater impact.

One day our toaster stopped working. Now that's not necessarily an earthshattering event. Toasters break all the time, and in the grand scheme of things, perhaps replacing a toaster isn't the most financially devastating event in our lives. But I wasn't ready to accept that option. You see, we had bought the toaster less than a month before. Yes, we could return it, but that would have been a hassle. The first thing we tried was plugging it into another outlet in a different part of the kitchen. And you know what, it worked. Problem solved? No, now we might be faced with a greater problem. We tried plugging another appliance into the previous outlet. Sure enough, there was no power. Immediately I talked to my wife about putting in a new outlet. If that didn't work, we would have to get an electrician to check the wiring. How much would that cost?

By this time it was getting too late to do anything, so we left the outlet and went to bed. As often happens, during the night another possibility occurred to me. In the morning, I checked the circuit box. Sure enough, one of the circuits was blown. I reset the breaker and tried the toaster again. This time it worked. Problem solved.

What is it about human beings that cause us to make things more complicated than they need to be? Most of what we do is predictable. We get up in the morning, have breakfast, go to work or school, come home, have dinner, hopefully have some time with our family, and then go to bed. I know your life may not exactly follow this routine, but even the exceptions usually have a degree of predictability. The reality is that most of life tends to be routine, and the exceptions are often brought about by trouble or even tragedy.

The same can be said of what we do on Sunday. We can vary what we do in our service to make it more interesting or to help hold our attention, and at times that's good. It can be helpful to our spiritual growth to experience our faith in different ways. But we can also let that tendency to make things complicated creep into our services, and, if we're not careful, the simple message can get lost in the complexity.

Today we're going to take the Lord's Supper. In one form or another Christians have been doing this for two thousand years. The ritual is simple, but the symbolism is so powerful. I think if the ritual were more complicated, the message just might get lost. Here it is in simple terms. We imitate the Last Supper by taking bread and fruit of the vine, and in doing that we remember the body and blood of our Lord. Nothing complicated, but if we understand it correctly, what we are doing can be very powerful.

We Are Not Worthy

As we prepare to take the Lord's Supper, we often come back to what Paul says in 1 Corinthians 11, and with good reason, because this is perhaps the earliest written account of what happened at the Last Supper. While we usually concentrate on verses 23-26, the verses following may have troubled some of us at one time or another.

Read 1 Cor. 11:27-29

Maybe you've heard a lesson about this passage and you understand intellectually that Paul is not referring to our being worthy to take the Lord's Supper. Rather, he is concerned with how we partake of the Lord's Supper — are we taking it in a worthy manner?

But it's that word "unworthy" that may cause us to question ourselves, no matter what the context. It's sometimes difficult to read the passage without the reality of that word hitting us. An unintended problem created by this difficulty is that it may actually cause us to do the very thing Paul warns us against. If we're distracted by focusing on our own spiritual unworthiness, we may very well end up taking the Lord's Supper in an unworthy manner, because we concentrate on ourselves, rather than on Christ.

Is there anything we can do to keep our emotional response from overpowering what we know intellectually Paul is really saying to us? I would suggest to you that the next time you are presented the Lord's Supper at a time you feel unworthy, that you remember that this is precisely what the Lord's Supper is supposed to represent. If we were worthy, the Lord's Supper would not even exist, because when we take it, we are remembering the very sacrifice that Jesus made, precisely because we are unworthy. His death on the cross was necessary, because we are sinful, unworthy creatures.

Understanding this should provide us with comfort, as we recognize that our insufficiency is no match for the love of Jesus. No, I am not worthy, and it is only when I recognize that reality that I can truly partake of the Lord's Supper in a worthy manner. After all, He said we should do this in memory of Him — not ourselves.

Spring and Resurrection

Suggestion — This is a good lesson to use during Spring. I wrote the first paragraph based on what I could see in my neighborhood. Obviously, your situation will be different. Write your own first paragraph in a way that will resonate with your congregation.

Have you bothered to look around this week? In our yard the grass is just beginning to turn green. Not surprising, you may think. After all, it's almost spring.

Of course we react that way only because we're used to seeing it. Imagine never having experienced changing seasons before. You watch the grass that was green in summer turn brown and dry during fall and winter. You might reasonably assume that it was all dead; nothing to do but dig it up and replant. But nature is resilient. Already the grass that just a couple of weeks ago looked brown, dry, and dead, is beginning to become green again.

Some of you know what it's like to come back from a seemingly hopeless situation, perhaps deserted by people who believed you were beyond hope. That's one thing we should remember about the Lord's Supper. Jesus died because He believed in hope. He died for us when we too were dead, seemingly beyond redemption. But Jesus knew that underneath all the sin, sorrow, and hopelessness lay the possibility of rebirth and renewal. It begins with His resurrection, for without that, nothing would be possible. But Jesus's resurrection merely provides the way for our rebirth, for a new life that is just as real and fruitful as the green grass is compared to the dried grass that was there during winter.

Maybe you're not experiencing the joy of that life right now. Maybe you think you're beyond hope. One message we get from the Lord's Supper is that not one of us is beyond the reach of His salvation. God would not allow His Son to die for nothing, and He did not create you for nothing. I don't know what is going on in your life right now, but I do know that new life is possible. That's the real promise of the gospel, and we should be reminded of it when we take the Lord's Supper.

The Aroma of Christ

Read 2 Corinthians 2:14-16

In this passage Paul refers to a custom that would have been quite familiar to people in the first century, a triumphal procession. When a Roman general won a great victory, the custom was for him to march down the streets of Rome in a grand procession, followed by his most trusted officers. At the rear of the procession would be captives he had conquered who were executed at the end of the ceremony. Using this imagery, Paul sees God in the aspect of Christ as the conqueror, leading the procession.

While there are different interpretations of Paul's symbolism, I wish to focus today on one aspect of it, his assertion in verse 15 that we are "the pleasing aroma of Christ." As the procession marched down the streets, clouds of incense would rise from censors lining the parade route. The incense was a reminder of the sweetness of victory. While the incense was a celebration of victory for the conquering general, it quite literally was the aroma of death for the captives, because they knew that the incense which celebrated the victory of the conqueror would result in their own deaths.

In a similar way, this passage reminds us that the gospel is perceived in different ways by different people. Consider how the Lord's Supper must appear to an agnostic or an atheist. For that person the Lord's Supper is nothing more than "eating bread and drinking grape juice or wine." Literally of course that is exactly what we do, and for unbelievers, it ends there. The Lord's Supper has no real meaning or purpose. They can see it, perhaps even participate in it, but it leads nowhere.

For Christians, however, the Lord's Supper can quite literally become the aroma of Christ, because it's a constant reminder that we have joined the triumphal procession that leads from the empty tomb to the very throne of God. For us, the taste of the bread and the smell of the fruit of the vine are reminders that we are both conquered and conquerors. By our surrender to the sovereignty of Christ, He has conquered, even killed our sinful nature. But He has also raised us to a new life, a life filled with the knowledge that we are children of the King of Kings and Lord of Lords.

Do Not Let Your Hearts Be Troubled

In John 14 Jesus is speaking to His disciples during the Last Supper. In verse 1 He says to them, "Do not let your hearts be troubled. You believe in God; believe also in me." This wasn't just an abstract theological teaching. There was reason for hearts to be troubled that night, more reason than even the disciples knew.

Jesus certainly had reason, because He knew that the next day He would be in a tomb. He also understood what He would have to endure before He could experience the relief of death. If we have any doubt that Jesus's heart was troubled, we only need accompany Him to Gethsemane.

The disciples had reason to be troubled. They knew there was danger. The preparations for the Passover had been made in secret. Then there had been all that talk of sorrow — of death, of burial, and resurrection. The disciples were understandably confused. Death, burial, resurrection? What was Jesus trying to teach them? They wished He wouldn't use parables, because often they didn't understand what He meant when He talked that way.

Jesus had even spoiled the Passover. Instead of reading the passages about Israel's deliverance from Egypt as tradition required, He had talked about the bread being His body, and the wine being His blood. Then tonight He spoke of going away and leaving them. But where was He going?

The Romans were everywhere; the Jewish leaders wanted Jesus dead. And here they were in the heart of

Jerusalem. Oh, yes, their hearts were troubled.

We don't often think about it, but the Lord's Supper began in a climate of fear. But looking back, the disciples would come to realize that at the other side of that fear was victory. However, it would not be until Jesus's resurrection that they would even begin to understand.

Suggestion — If desired, you may read the comments below at the same time as those above; however, you might wish to wait and read them just before the fruit of the vine is passed.

How about you? Has your heart ever been troubled? The answer to that question is obvious isn't it? Perhaps you're troubled right now. What is it for you?

• An illness you've been fighting for a long time, which drains the strength from the body, and the life from the spirit.

• Are you struggling with grief over the loss of a loved one whose presence you miss almost more than you can bear?

• Perhaps you're dealing with an uncertain financial future that leaves you wondering if tomorrow will be provided for.

• Maybe it's a deeply troubled family situation that other people don't even know about, or a sin that has you in its grip and will not let go.

To whatever troubles your heart today, Jesus gives the same answer — Himself. He took upon Himself all of the struggles, the uncertainty, the heartbreak that come with being human. He overcame them — even death itself, if only to make us understand that God is still in control and there is so much more than the struggles of this life.

Jesus doesn't make any grand promises; He just asks us to trust Him. He has the power to take that troubled heart and calm it, even if Gethsemane still awaits us. We have His promise that He will overcome whatever troubles us. "Do not let your hearts be troubled." He means that for us too.

The Real Use of Power

While the date August 9, 1974, may not immediately ring a bell, I suspect that almost everyone old enough can remember where they were that night.

Suggestion — If you are old enough to remember, talk about what you were doing the night described below.

While everyone knew what Richard Nixon would say, it was still hard to believe that it had come to this. A president of the United States was resigning from office in order to avoid almost certain impeachment for covering up, if not actually authorizing criminal activity.

We've all heard the saying, "power corrupts," and since 1974 we have witnessed many more examples of that principle, and it doesn't just apply to government. Social and even religious leaders have been shown to be incapable of withstanding the allure of power, and we've seen many of them fall.

Sadly, the same can occur in families. Too often we see examples of abuse that come from one member, often the husband and father, seeing his role as one of power, rather than responsibility.

What a different view of power is presented by God, the one truly absolute power that does exist. Jesus acknowledged that power, when He told His disciples that, if He chose to, He could call twelve legions of angels to rescue Him from the hands of the authorities who had come to arrest Him. But Jesus recognized that this was not how His power was intended to be used.

One source of conflict for Jesus resulted from His very different view of power. Jesus was not killed because He was the Messiah. He was killed because He wasn't the Messiah the people wanted. For the Jewish leaders, the Messiah would be the one sent by God, with the strength to overthrow the Romans, and then give them the power to control the world. You see, they weren't against power; they just wanted to be on top. For Jesus, power meant servanthood, sacrifice, and ultimately a cross.

Power did not corrupt Jesus, because He understood how it was really intended to be used — not for our own gain, but for the benefit of others. And He demonstrated that most clearly by dying for us.

Today as we take the Lord's Supper, we're reminded that Jesus gave up all the power that was rightfully His in order to save us. Let's remember that and resolve to follow His example in our own lives.

D-Day

Suggestion — This presentation can be more effective if you do the following. Prior to the Lord's Supper, have the song leader lead the congregation in the first two verses of "It is Finished." At that point, the presider can present the comments below.

Jesus often spoke in parables, using illustrations from peoples' lives to help them understand His teaching. I want to do something similar today. I'm going to relate a story from our not too distant history that I believe will present a powerful image of what Jesus has done for us.

Suggestion — This presentation can be made even more powerful if you project a picture of a landing craft heading for the shore. This type of visual imagery can aid the congregation in imagining themselves in the boat. Images are readily available on the internet. Just be conscious of any copyright restrictions on using images.

Imagine for a moment that it's early morning, June 6, 1944, a date that has come to be known as D-Day. You're on a landing craft that holds about thirty people, and you're headed for Omaha Beach. Now don't just listen to my words. Try to imagine yourself in that boat. You're cold, you're wet, you're seasick — and you are absolutely terrified.

As you get closer to the beach, shells from artillery onshore begin falling around you. One of them lands so close, the force of the explosion almost capsizes the boat. In just a few minutes, the small ramp in the front will drop open, and all thirty of you will have to scramble through the opening, knowing that machine guns from the beach will be firing right at that very spot. And you wonder how you can possibly stay alive for another five minutes. Have you put yourself in that awful place? Have you tried to imagine what that must have felt like?

Now, at this time, I'm going to change history, by describing something that did not happen. Imagine for a moment that suddenly the firing from the beach stops. At almost the same time the guns from the ships offshore also fall silent. You receive a message to hold your position. For what seems like an eternity there is an eerie silence. Then you receive another message from offshore. "The Germans have surrendered. Return to the ship. The war is over."

Of course that did not happen. But can you imagine the relief you would feel, knowing you would not have to make that deadly assault? And have you ever considered that something very like that has happened to us? Did you notice the words of the song we sang?

It is finished! The battle is over,
It is finished! There'll be no more war;
It is finished! The end of the conflict,
It is finished, and Jesus is Lord.

And truly that is what Jesus did for us. As horrible as Omaha Beach was on that day, we were confronting a far worse fate. They had to contend with the possibility of physical death; we were facing eternal death. But because Jesus loved us so much, He took upon Himself that battle and won it. Jesus faced Satan and hell itself, so we would not have to.

We're now going to sing the fifth verse of "It is Finished" before we take the Lord's supper. As you sing, think of the words, and consider the reality of what Jesus has done for us.

Suggestion — At this point, the presider may sit down, while the congregation sings verse 5 of "It is Finished." After that, continue on with the Lord's Supper.

Why Do You Call Me Good?

Read Mark 10:17-22

In the movie *Forrest Gump*, Forrest is waiting for a bus. At one point, he talks about the time he met Elvis Presley, who of course came to be known as "the King." When Forrest finishes talking about Elvis, he says, "Some years later, that handsome young man who they called 'The King', well he sung too many songs. He had himself a heart attack or something. Must be hard being the king." I believe this image describes the man in the story we just read about. He was trying to live up to expectations that no one could achieve.

As Mark describes it, when He encountered the man, Jesus was on His way to Jerusalem, knowing that He was going to His death. This story seems especially applicable to those of us who were raised in a good Christian home, who grew up with Bible class, regular worship services, Vacation Bible School, and all the rest. In his Jewish culture that seems to describe this man. Sins? What sins? I've kept all the commandments since childhood. What else do I have to do?

So Jesus confronts this man head-on. He had called Jesus good, but from what he said, it seems like this man felt that he was the one who was good. In order to try to get the man to confront his misconception, Jesus says the obvious, although the man doesn't grasp it. "No one is good — except God alone." I wonder if there was a bit of a twinkle in Jesus's eye as He said this, knowing that this man had no idea that God was exactly the One to whom he was speaking. How could Jesus have explained to this man that his sins were black enough that they required that Jesus continue His journey to Jerusalem and there die because of people just like this man?

And if we're not careful, we too may miss the point. When we take the Lord's Supper, we acknowledge that what Jesus said of this man is just as true for us. "No one is good — except God alone." You see, we're just like this man. Oh, it may not be wealth for us, but it's something, something we are unwilling to give up. And so, Jesus had to die, for this man certainly, but just as much for you and for me. Because we are not good, not one of us.

As we take the Lord's Supper today, don't fall into the same trap this man did, by thinking that we too have kept the commandments since our youth. Only if we can stop pretending we're good, will we be able to recognize the One who is good and gave His life for us, so that we can have a goodness, not of our own, but the goodness that comes through being in Him. Because, "No one is good — except God alone."

Living the Kingdom of God

What does being a Christian mean to you? When you think about being a Christian, what sort of images come to mind? Do you think first of all about what we're doing here right now? How should we view what we do in this building today? Is that what the church is all about?

I would suggest that if we equate church with the rituals and teachings that we associate with our meetings here, we have a very short-sided view. It treats all that we're doing today as an end in itself.

Now the other extreme can be dangerous as well. A lot of people these days have become very critical of organized churches, assemblies, and all that go with them. I don't share that view. I think what we're doing today is very important, and it would be a tragedy with serious consequences if we were to stop meeting together. At the same time, if we fall into the trap of seeing what we do here as the primary measure of our Christianity, we totally misunderstand what God intends for His church to be.

Jesus often pictures the kingdom of God as it applies to our lives here on earth. He says it's like searching for a lost coin, finding a pearl, a tiny seed that grows into a large bush. It's not seen as much in a building as it is out in the world. The kingdom of God is not demonstrated nearly as effectively by reading a scripture, leading a prayer, or presenting a devotional before the Lord's Supper, as it is in sitting with a lonely person, visiting someone in the hospital, or taking a meal to a person who needs it.

On one of the social media sites a minister told why he has stopped calling himself a Christian. His reasons are valid to a degree and need to be considered. He pointed out that the word "Christian" has come to have negative connotations. The world often equates it with hypocrisy, self-righteousness, hatred, and intolerance. Make no mistake; there's enough truth in those charges to make us all feel uncomfortable. But I disagree with his response. If that's the way the world perceives Christians — even more, if that is the reality too many Christians portray to the world — then I would suggest it is all the more important that we let the world know we are Christians, so they can see that this negative vision of the church is flawed and doesn't reflect reality for so many people who wear the name of Christ with humility and try to live out the implications of their faith in their lives.

Jesus did not die so we could meet together and worship each week. He died to make God king of our lives — today, tomorrow, and throughout all eternity. We take the bread and the fruit of the vine to remind us that the kingdom of God is within each one of us. And it is to be lived out every day of our lives.

Symbol and Reality

The bread "represents" Jesus's body. The fruit of the vine "represents" Jesus's blood." How many of you have heard something like this? Now I would like someone to tell me where in the Bible it tells us that.

The reality is that the New Testament presents the significance of the Lord's Supper in more graphic language. Matthew describes it in these words. "[26]While they were eating, Jesus took bread, and when he had given thanks, he broke it and gave it to his disciples, saying, 'Take and eat; this is my body.' [27]Then he took a cup, and when he had given thanks, he gave it to them, saying, 'Drink from it, all of you. [28]This is my blood of the covenant, which is poured out for many for the forgiveness of sins.'" (Matthew 26:26-28).

There are some people who have taken these words literally, believing that the elements of the Lord's Supper actually become the body and blood of Christ. While we may not interpret Jesus's words literally, we would do well to recognize the reality that Jesus was trying to impress on His disciples and perhaps on us as well.

Part of the problem arises, because it is easy to misunderstand the nature of both symbol and reality. We've become so accustomed to the Age of Reason that we virtually define reality by one of our five senses, and if we can't see, hear, taste, smell, or touch something, it isn't real. The opposite is also believed to be true. If we can experience something, then it must be the reality. I'm not sure either of those pictures tells the whole story.

In Jesus's day, the Jews felt they understood the reality of sacrifice. They saw animals being slaughtered at the temple. They heard the squeal of the animal and smelled the odor of the blood. Sacrifice was real.

But Jesus, as He so often does, turns their reality around. What Jesus is telling His disciples — what He would have us understand — is that all those sacrifices were symbols. Jesus on the cross shows us the reality that all those sacrifices symbolized.

Do we believe that? Do we really understand that Jesus's death on the cross was in reality the one sacrifice to which all the millions of earlier sacrifices pointed? Or do we see Jesus's death as just another symbol?

Read all that Paul promises us in Romans, chapters 6 through 8. He talks about our being crucified with Christ. He tells us that in that process the old man dies, but is raised to a new life, energized by the Holy Spirit living within us. Do we believe that, or is it just another symbol?

It all comes down to this. If all of this is just a symbol, then we are without hope, because nothing has really changed. The power of the gospel is the assurance that, although the Lord's Supper uses symbols, it represents a reality that you and I can live every single day. Make no mistake, it is reality we celebrate today, not just a symbol.

God Invades the Everyday

Think for a moment about how you would finish this sentence. "I experience the reality of God most commonly through—" How would you answer that question?

[Pause to give people a moment to think.]

Was the Sunday morning worship the first thing that came to mind? Perhaps you're a Sunday school teacher, and you see that as your most effective spiritual gift. Maybe you're involved in Christian works that help others.

These are certainly areas in which our faith can and should express itself. Indeed, I can't imagine Christianity without these expressions of faith and so many more. The danger comes when we compartmentalize our faith into specifically religious actions.

We know that Jesus was regularly involved in the religious practices of His day, but these are not how the gospel writers normally present Him. The gospels show Jesus attending a wedding, riding in a boat, having dinner (often with those the religious people felt He shouldn't). And it's in these settings that Jesus acted and from which much of His teaching comes.

Even the Lord's Supper is derived from a meal Jesus shared with His disciples. Yes, it was probably the Passover, a religious meal. But that just illustrates the reality that this is what God has been doing all along, invading our lives, not just through religious services and rituals, but meeting with us in the everyday affairs of life, where perhaps we most need to see God at work.

So we should view the Lord's Supper as just one way in which God makes Himself known in the commonplace routines of life. He can make anything holy, whether a simple meal, a walk in the woods, playing golf with a buddy, or even the painful death of a loved one. If we see God acting only in this building, our God is too small. He wants to be part of every aspect of our lives.

If you have any doubt of that, consider for a moment that the most profound expression of our faith that He left us has its origins in a shared meal and is expressed today in a bit of bread and a cup of juice or wine. So the Lord's Supper should remind us that we worship a God whose holiness isn't experienced just in great cathedrals with stirring music. Rather, He is big enough to share in the everyday aspects of our lives, even death itself, so that His transforming power can touch us at the center of whatever need we have — right now, tomorrow, and every day of our lives.

Freedom is Not Free

Suggestion — This message is designed to be used just before or after July 4.

This week we celebrate Independence Day, when we recognize the founding of our nation. It's interesting how we have perceived that at different times in our history.

Since its beginning in 1888, The *National Geographic Magazine* has provided a window into our world. Often the advertisements are just as revealing as the articles. Just one example is in the March 1943 issue, a time when the United States was deeply engaged in World War II. Union Pacific Railroad ran an advertisement, describing how they were transporting immense quantities of fresh fruit and vegetables to both military supply depots, as well as civilian markets. The ad ends with the statement, "It's a patriotic duty for *all Americans* to keep fit. Eat vitamins for victory!" Whatever you may think about that ad, it clearly shows how dedicated the entire country was to winning the war, and it served as a reminder that the cost of victory would be high.

There is another phrase you may have heard — "Freedom is not free." Certainly that has been true for our nation, and those who have served in war, as well as their families, are especially aware of the high cost of freedom.

The Lord's Supper reminds us that our freedom from sin was not free either. It was procured for you and me at a terrible cost. We celebrate the freedom we have in this country, as well we should. Let's also recognize the freedom we have in Christ — freedom from law, freedom from the slavery to sin, but also the freedom to live a new life — a life filled with joy today, hope for tomorrow, and the promise of ultimate eternal life. But let us never forget the cost at which Jesus secured that new life for us. Today we remember both the new life we enjoy, as well as the cost at which that life was purchased.

The True Nature of Sacrifice

I suspect most of us are familiar with the story in Genesis 22 in which Abraham is told to sacrifice his son Isaac. As Abraham prepares to kill Isaac, an angel stays his hand, and a ram is substituted. There are a number of lessons we can get from this story. Today I want to focus on only one.

Human sacrifice was pervasive in the ancient world. In various cultures it was common to sacrifice slaves, prisoners of war, even a person's own child. Perhaps you've been told that the message God is trying to tell us in this story is that He does not want human sacrifice. If we view the story in the context of the culture of the ancient world, that is obviously true. But have you ever paused to ask why that is? In the ancient world human sacrifice was gruesome, bloody, and almost always involuntary. The person being sacrificed was not asked if he or she consented to it. Their desires were of no concern.

The other aspect of sacrifice (even animal sacrifice under the Law of Moses) was that it was inherently a selfish act. Another person or animal was sacrificed, so that the person offering the sacrifice could gain or prosper in some way.

The true purpose of the story in Genesis isn't to warn us against human sacrifice. Rather it's meant to take us to a new understanding of sacrifice. The true nature of sacrifice is shown by Jesus as He voluntarily offered Himself as the ultimate human sacrifice, not selfishly for His own benefit, but as the perfect expression of love for us.

That concept is repeated by the apostle Paul, when he wrote in Romans 12:1 "Therefore, I urge you, brothers and sisters, in view of God's mercy, to offer your bodies as a living sacrifice, holy and pleasing to God — this is your true and proper worship." So, we can see that God does in fact call for human sacrifice, but how different from the way the peoples of the ancient world understood sacrifice. In fact, how different from how our culture understands it now. Isn't it routine in the corporate world to advance oneself at the expense of someone else? We've all known husbands or wives who were more than willing to force their spouse to give up their own desires and dreams, so that the other party could get what they wanted.

You see, God's view of sacrifice is so different from ours. Sacrifice is first of all a sacrifice of ourselves. It means giving up what I want for someone else's good. It also includes a recognition that our very lives are meant to be one continuing sacrifice that we give in order to advance God's kingdom on this earth. And we remember that sacrifice in the bread and fruit of the vine. Jesus gave Himself, not someone else. He did it for our good, not His own. And He calls us to follow that same example.

He Understands Fear

Have you ever been afraid? That's a silly question, isn't it? Each of us at one time or another has been afraid. Sometimes fear can be about relatively small problems. Will I do well on that pop quiz tomorrow morning? Am I ready for my mother-in-law's visit? But sometimes fear takes on a much more ominous form. Parents anxiously waiting for the surgeon to come out and tell them how their child's surgery went. A soldier, staring into a terrifying darkness. Oh yes, in one form or another, each of us has to deal with fear.

Jesus understands that, because He too had to wrestle with fear. If you doubt that, just listen to how Matthew describes Him. "³⁷He took Peter and the two sons of Zebedee along with him, and he began to be sorrowful and troubled. ³⁸Then he said to them, 'My soul is overwhelmed with sorrow to the point of death. Stay here and keep watch with me.'" (Matt. 26:37, 38).

The writer of Hebrews says it in a more general way. "For we do not have a high priest who is unable to empathize with our weaknesses, but we have one who has been tempted in every way, just as we are — yet he did not sin." (Hebrews 4:15).

So what is the point today? We should understand that fear does not necessarily indicate a lack of faith. Jesus goes on to express to the Father His faith in Him and in the Father's plan for Jesus. At the same time, Jesus did not want to endure the horrors He knew were coming, any more than you or I would. And that kind of fear is not a sin. Actually, Jesus's fear should provide comfort to us when we too are facing a dark situation and we find ourselves afraid. That's just one of the ways that Jesus is able to, as Hebrews says, "empathize with our weaknesses." There is so much involved in remembering what Jesus did for us, and there are a multitude of lessons to be learned from it. Right now though, take at least a moment to be grateful that, whatever you are struggling with, Jesus understands.

Suffering Is Witness

We all know what it means to be a witness to something, even if we've never had to testify in court. In English the very word "witness" implies something we know firsthand. In other words, we cannot be a witness about something we have not experienced directly.

That distinction is important, because sometimes we confuse teaching someone the Bible with witnessing. I don't want to minimize in any way the importance of knowing what the Bible says. But I suspect that many times sharing how the gospel has changed my own life can be even more effective at helping another person believe that Christ may do the same for them.

In Greek the word that is normally translated as "testimony" or "witness" is "*martúrion.*" It's the word from which we get the English word "martyr." There may be a hint as to why that connection exists in 2 Timothy 1:8 where we read, "So do not be ashamed of the testimony about our Lord or of me his prisoner. Rather, join with me in suffering for the gospel, by the power of God." In this passage, testifying is linked to suffering for the gospel. That threat may have been more real to the early Christians than it probably is for us in twenty-first century America, but it's a concept we should consider carefully.

If we're ever tempted to doubt the power of suffering, we only need to consider the example of Jesus. Much of Jesus's teaching is preserved for us in the New Testament. It's inspiring and has the ability to change our lives if we apply it. But without Jesus's redemptive act of suffering, His teachings might be considered just one more example of wise sayings from ancient times, perhaps on a level with Plato or Aristotle. But because Jesus was willing to suffer for what He had done and taught, we see Him in a different light. Jesus's suffering gives validity to His life and His teaching as nothing else could.

And that leaves us with an example to follow. We shouldn't manufacture suffering, but we are expected to have a faith and an integrity that is willing to suffer in whatever way may be required of us, recognizing that this may be the most powerful witness we can have. If there is any encouragement for us, it is in the last part of 2 Timothy 1:8 where we are told that we do not endure suffering by our own strength or will, but "by the power of God." Just as Jesus ultimately depended on the Father to see Him through what He had to endure, so we too must rely on the power of the Holy Spirit when we are faced with suffering (or witnessing) for our faith. But never doubt the power that can come from being willing to do that.

Someone Pays for Every Gift

Have you ever been given a surprise birthday party, one that you didn't know was planned? How did it make you feel? Embarrassed probably. If there were gifts involved, did you enjoy receiving them? Often we seem to possess a curious resistance to accepting gifts. Most of us feel uncomfortable when someone gives us a gift. I'm not sure every culture shares this strange reluctance, and I wonder why we do.

Perhaps part of our aversion to accepting gifts comes from an independent streak that overall has served America well. Standing on our own, making it without help, is seen in our culture as a virtue. And I believe that sense of self-reliance has been to some degree responsible for the accomplishments this country has made throughout our relatively short history.

Perhaps that's why we don't like to accept gifts. A gift is something we didn't earn on our own. By definition, a gift is something that is *given* to us, and to that extent it reduces our own self-reliance, because we know that no gift is free. Even if the person giving it did not pay for it, someone did. Someone pays the price for every gift.

And despite what we like to think, none of us are completely self-reliant. Each of us has at some time depended on someone else for something. That's just reality, and I'm convinced there are no exceptions.

And so we gather here to partake of the Lord's Supper. Are there some of you here today unconvinced about who paid the price?

"I'm as good as the next guy."

"I've done too much; no one can forgive me."

"What do bread and grape juice have to do with anything?"

Yes, it takes many forms, but our reluctance to receive gifts, while a virtue in some respects, can be deadly in others.

You may have heard the argument, "Would a drowning person reject a rope thrown to him by someone else?" Perhaps it's an old argument, but isn't that really what we're talking about. The excuses are many, but they sound shallow when we really consider them. Someone pays the price for every gift. When we partake of the Lord's Supper, we acknowledge that we have received an incomparable gift which we could never have earned on our own. We also remember that Jesus paid the price for the unparalleled gifts of forgiveness and eternal life.

Remembering

Suggestion — You can personalize this devotional by taking an experience in your own life. For example, I used a time when we were moving out of state and how that brought back memories of all the good times we had experienced that made the move bittersweet. A personal touch will allow each member of the congregation to do the same thing in their own minds, and thus make the illustration all the richer.

Read 1 Cor. 11:24-25

Have you ever had a period in your life during which memories from the past came flooding back? Perhaps a child's graduation or marriage, or a time when you had to leave the city in which you had lived for many years caused you to reflect on all the circumstances that had brought you to this point in your life. I believe it was C. S. Lewis who observed that memory is the final and most permanent part of any experience. Significant events have the power to impress on us how important memories really are.

In the passage from 1 Corinthians we just read, Paul tells of the instance during the Last Supper when Jesus emphasized to His disciples just how important it was to remember that night and the days that were to follow. The Lord's Supper helped the disciples understand that those dark days were not the end. They were followed by an eternity of hope.

Remembering Jesus's death in the Lord's Supper can strengthen us as well. It helps us to focus on the truly important when the pressures of the world tempt us to tune it out. No, we cannot share the memory of the Last Supper; we weren't there. However, that's one of the blessings of the Christian life. As we look back at how God has entered our lives, in the trials, as well as the good times, we can see how He has used all of our experiences to mold us into the people we have become. While we cannot share the actual memory of the Last Supper two thousand years ago, we do remember how God has worked in our lives in the past and continues to do so even now. So today, in a real sense, we have forged our own memories with the living Christ.

To Whom Shall We Go?

Read John 6:66-68

Jesus had gone from entertaining the crowds with bread and miracles to giving them some difficult teaching. The response was perhaps as discouraging as it was predictable. John tells us that many of Jesus's disciples stopped following Him. As long as the crowds were entertained and fed, they remained with Jesus, but when He began making demands, they lost interest. How tragically characteristic of our world today.

This is one of those passages that I wish I could have heard Jesus speaking. I think I can almost hear the disappointment in His voice as He asks His disciples, "[67]You do not want to leave too, do you?"

I find Peter's response interesting on two different levels. The first is that once again Peter gets it. Despite Peter's reputation, he was right far more often than he was wrong. If Peter was impetuous, it was only because his faith was simple, direct, and imminently practical. Jesus had asked a question. Notice Peter's answer. "[68]Lord, to whom shall we go? You have the words of eternal life."

Also, Peter's faith isn't based on platitudes or promises of good fortune. He knows too much to see God as a grandfather figure handing out candy. He realizes that following Jesus is going to be hard, although as yet Peter has no idea just how hard it really will be. For Peter it's simply a matter of weighing alternatives, only to find there really are no alternatives worth considering.

Jesus faced a similar dilemma Himself. In the garden, facing a horrible death, even He looked for another way out, only to face the realization that there really was no other option open to Him.

And so it is for us as well. Make no mistake, Jesus requires of us every bit as much as He required of Peter. We may not have to be crucified like Peter, but in some form or another, Jesus still requires of us our very lives. There will be times when the demands seem more than we can bear, or when tragedy seems ready to overwhelm us. At those times, Jesus seems to be asking us the same question — "[67]You do not want to leave too, do you?" And at those times, Peter's answer may be the only one we can give. "[68]Lord, to whom shall we go? You have the words of eternal life."

We're going to take the Lord's Supper now, when we remember His death on the cross for us. Let it also serve as a reminder that Jesus asks nothing of us that He has not also required of Himself.

Do I Matter?

Do I matter? When I leave this earth, will my life have made any difference? Have you ever asked yourself these questions?

Suggestion — I have written the next paragraph from my own perspective, being in my 60s. I suggest you rewrite it to fit your own situation and experiences. Let this paragraph reflect who you are.

I have to admit that I am much nearer to the end of my life on this earth than the beginning. I've had occasion to look back and see what I've accomplished with my life. If I choose, I can view the negatives — all the things I failed to achieve. At this point I suspect it's extremely unlikely that I will become President of the United States. I doubt that I will ever be a pro basketball star *[This was added for humor. I am very short.]*, and I can assure you that I will not be a professional singer.

While we can laugh about such things, I suspect the reality may be more serious. Have you ever asked yourself if you mattered, if you were important, if it would even make a difference that you ever lived?

We live in a culture that worships the exceptional — the sports figure, the movie star, the business tycoon — the rich, the famous. But who influences society more; a glamorous movie star, or a teacher who molds the life of a child; a research scientist who discovers a new treatment for a disease, or the one who shares the gospel message with someone else who is lost in every meaning of the term?

Far too many people look at themselves, see nothing worthwhile, and become discouraged or even give in to despair. Yet our Lord speaks forcefully to that attitude. Matthew 10:29-31 reads "Are not two sparrows sold for a penny? Yet not one of them will fall to the ground outside your Father's care. [30]And even the very hairs of your head are all numbered. [31]So don't be afraid; you are worth more than many sparrows."

How much are you worth? We only need to look at the cross to see how much God thinks you are worth. Today we remember Jesus and try to understand something of the magnitude of His love. At the same time, take a moment to consider that He would not have gone through it unless He believed that you are worth it — that you matter. And if God considers you worthwhile, you are valued by the only one whose opinion counts. Remember Christ as we take the Lord's Supper. Remember His love. But also, remember that He loves you specifically. You do matter.

What Is Love?

Since the Middle Ages, the subject of love has dominated almost every aspect of our culture — our art, our poetry, our music. And the word is viewed differently in various languages. The Greeks tried to analyze and dissect various kinds of love, so they ended up with four different words that English translates simply as "love." We can do that, because we "love" almost everything. We love our spouse, our children, a crisp fall day, a beautiful symphony.

Ask our teenagers about love. Can the rest of us remember that far back? At that age, love possesses an intensity that we who are older sometimes struggle to hold onto. However, as we do grow older, we experience love in more challenging ways. You can see it in the spouse who supports you when you lose your job, the nervous anxiety you feel as the nurse takes your child down to have his or her tonsils removed, the sense of loss as you stand before the grave of your father or mother.

Obviously love is not exclusively a happy feeling. But we shouldn't concentrate on times of sorrow either. Love is the glue that binds people together in all the varied experiences of life. It's what makes us shout with joy when our child makes a goal. Love is Thanksgiving dinner that is so rich, not just because of the abundance of food, but because we share it with family. Love is the handmade valentine that is beyond price, because my child made it.

In the comic strip *Peanuts*, that great philosopher and

theologian, Linus, affirms, "I love mankind; it's people I can't stand." I suspect more people than Linus have felt that way. But John says, "[9]Anyone who claims to be in the light but hates a brother or sister is still in the darkness. [10]Anyone who loves their brother and sister lives in the light, and there is nothing in them to make them stumble." (1 John 2:9-10). And that's where the true meaning of love is shown. The truth is that we cannot say we love mankind, if we don't love people. I would suggest to you that real love is not about us. Love is entirely about someone else; doing what is good for them at any cost. Jesus showed us what real love looks like, and we remember His sacrificial love every Sunday. Today, as you contemplate that love, why not resolve to make that same love a part of your life? That's perhaps the best way to respond to what Jesus did for us.

Hope

As it relates to Christianity, hope isn't always perceived in a positive way. Perhaps that's because hope seems to imply a lack of faith. Why hope for what we want from God? Shouldn't we just believe He will provide what we need? Maybe it's because sometimes hope can be a roundabout way of saying we can't really be sure of our relationship with God.

"Will you go to Heaven?"

"I hope so."

But the New Testament presents hope in a much more positive way. Listen to just a few verses in which Paul uses the word.

Romans 5:2b-5. "[2]And we boast in the hope of the glory of God. [3]Not only so, but we also glory in our sufferings, because we know that suffering produces perseverance; [4]perseverance, character; and character, hope. [5]And hope does not put us to shame, because God's love has been poured out into our hearts through the Holy Spirit, who has been given to us."

Romans 15:13. "May the God of hope fill you with all joy and peace as you trust in him, so that you may overflow with hope by the power of the Holy Spirit."

1 Thessalonians 1:3. "We remember before our God and Father your work produced by faith, your labor prompted by love, and your endurance inspired by hope in our Lord Jesus Christ."

Other verses could be read, but these should provide enough encouragement to us.

We all know what it's like to hope for something. I hope I get the job. I hope the test results are negative. I hope she says, "Yes." And this kind of hope isn't wishful thinking or fantasy. Rather it's the anticipation of experiencing the reality of that for which we strive. How would my life change if I did get that job? Consider the relief if the tests show I don't have a fatal illness. Imagine my happiness if the woman of my dreams did say "Yes." Some of us don't have to imagine that, because it has come true for us. For others, the hope is still out there to provide comfort and encouragement.

For those of us who are God's children, hope just means the promise hasn't been fulfilled yet. At the Last Supper Jesus lived in hope. It wasn't that He doubted the outcome, but He anticipated the fulfillment, when all the pain, anguish, and sorrow would have been accomplished, and redemption had become reality.

And so we too live in hope, not a fanciful, desperate longing, but the reasoned assurance that what we hope for will in time become a living reality, just as it did for Jesus. By the way, remember Paul's final verdict in 1 Corinthians 13:13 "And now these three remain: faith, hope and love. But the greatest of these is love." What will remain for us to hope for in eternity? I don't know, but one day I *hope* to find out.

The Most Shoplifted Book

Do you have any idea what is the most shoplifted book in the world? It's the Bible. At first that may seem strange. Why would anyone commit an immoral (not to mention an illegal) act in order to obtain a book that, at its heart, attempts to help us live moral lives?

As strange as this contradiction might at first appear, I wonder if it says something fundamental about us as human beings. Are we so certain we aren't guilty of something very similar? We read the Bible to help us learn how we should live, but in more instances than we care to acknowledge, we either ignore its teachings or try to explain them away. Why do we read the Bible, if we don't intend to live by it?

I would suggest to you that, to a degree that is what it means to be a fallen human being. Paul put it this way in Romans 7:21-24. "[21]So I find this law at work: Although I want to do good, evil is right there with me. [22]For in my inner being I delight in God's law; [23]but I see another law at work in me, waging war against the law of my mind and making me a prisoner of the law of sin at work within me. [24]What a wretched man I am! Who will rescue me from this body that is subject to death?"

Is there anyone here today who can't identify with Paul's dilemma? We've all wrestled with that kind of moral tug-of-war, and, strange as it may sound, it may be that the more we want to live a spiritual life, the more we struggle with these problems.

Of course, Paul provides us with the solution in the

next verse. "Thanks be to God, who delivers me through Jesus Christ our Lord!" And that ultimately is the only answer that works. There is no self-help program for sin, because part of the enslaving power of sin is its ability to make us incapable of changing on our own, no matter how much we might wish to do so. The good news is that Jesus fixed the sin problem. Yes, He took our sins on Himself, so that we do not have to pay the penalty for our sins. But He did even more than that. If we look back to Romans 6 and forward to Romans 8, we also find that Jesus's death accomplished at least two other things. First, when we are crucified with Christ, the old man of sin is killed, destroying its hold over us. But equally important is the new life Paul talks about in Romans 8, a life energized by the Holy Spirit living within us.

So now, because of the death of Christ, we have supernatural help to live the way we hopefully want to live. Maybe by the way we live our lives we're doing the equivalent of shoplifting a Bible, but it doesn't matter anymore. We can now read it and apply it, quite literally with a new Spirit, helping us every day to live the way we really want to live.

Thomas — Faith vs. Doubt

Read John 20:24-29

Many of us are familiar with this story, and traditionally Thomas has been portrayed as lacking faith. But in some ways this story gives us more questions than answers. What about Thomas? Should he be forever labeled as "doubting Thomas"?

Was Thomas's faith really less than that of the other disciples? They didn't believe in the resurrection at first either, and even on this occasion John tells us they had the door locked, because they were afraid. I don't see a lot of faith demonstrated in that room.

What about you? Have you ever said in your heart, "If only I could see, I would never have a problem believing"? The evidence suggests this isn't true. If it were, why did the disciples, who had seen the resurrected Jesus, still bolt the door? Is it possible we can learn something about ourselves from Thomas?

Is doubt the "unforgivable sin" we have sometimes been led to think it is? Is it possible that doubt is not necessarily the absence of faith, but rather an opportunity for our faith to be tested and even strengthened?

Doubt may be like a skydiver making his first parachute jump. He has taken all the classes, learned the statistics, and practiced the safety precautions. He understands that the parachute is designed to give him a safe landing. But now it's time to step out of the airplane. Does he have faith in his instructor? Does he believe that all he has learned is true? Of course he does. But now he has to weigh all that against actually stepping out of the plane. That's where doubt and faith intersect. If the would be skydiver pulls back and refuses to leave the plane, doubt will never go away, and it will become more and more difficult to generate the faith required to try again. But if he masters his doubt enough to step out of the plane, the sight of the parachute opening and that first safe landing will strengthen his faith and make each subsequent jump easier.

What about you? Are you paralyzed by doubt? Why is that? Is it because God has proven untrustworthy, or is it because you have never been willing to overcome the doubt enough to step out with the faith that God is there to catch you?

Doubt and faith. I'm convinced we must face the one before we can truly claim the other. The Lord's Supper provides an opportunity for us to examine our faith, because it brings into focus the one event upon which that faith must rest. The words, "He is risen" are at the heart of our faith. Where is your faith today?

Triumph Over Failure

Suggestion — In the first paragraph below I give an example of failure in my own life. Make this reading personal by writing your own first paragraph, giving an example of failure in your life. It does not need to be a huge or embarrassing failure. It can even be funny. But an example from your own experience can help the audience identify with the subject.

I never was good at sports when I was growing up. The reason is simple; I had two older brothers who could cream me at anything I attempted. My definition of success was getting through the game without any broken bones or major bruises. It seemed prudent to focus my efforts in other directions.

How about you? Have you ever failed at anything? I can't say for sure, but I'm fairly confident that right now each of you can remember something in the past that didn't turn out the way you wanted it to. Failure is a part of the human condition. We've all experienced it, in small ways, and probably bigger things as well.

But success and failure don't always look the same to other people. Jesus's contemporaries must have felt He had failed. After all, His ministry had ended with a horrifying death on a cross. Not much to build on there. Even His disciples had given up. Their main concern was staying out of the way of the authorities to keep from suffering the same fate as Jesus. But in the very act of taking the Lord's Supper we affirm our confidence that

Jesus did not fail, that His death, a sign of defeat at first, became the most significant victory in all of human history.

The good news for us is that, because of that "successful failure," you and I can experience the ultimate victory that we could never achieve on our own. I don't know where your life is right now. I can't see the failures of the past or the struggles of the present. But one thing I can say with absolute assurance. Whatever you have done, however you may have failed, there is no one here today who is beyond the power of God to forgive — and to heal. Jesus turned failure to victory. He has done it for millions throughout the centuries. He can do the same for you as well.

Our Debt of Faith

I want you to think for a moment about the source of your faith. Where did that faith come from? Many of us were fortunate enough to have Christian parents, who modeled their own faith from the time we were born. For others, your faith may have been the result of a long and difficult journey. Whatever the source of your faith, I hope you can recognize that, for all of us, faith goes back much further than our immediate family or even the specific circumstances of our life.

We have a rich heritage that stretches back almost two thousand years. I want you to picture something in your mind. Let's use the front of the auditorium to help visualize it. All the way over to my right, I want you to picture the apostle John standing there. No, I don't know what he looked like either; you may picture him any way you wish. Just to the left of John stands a man named Polycarp. Polycarp probably knew John when he was an old man, and Polycarp was a young man. Next to Polycarp is a man named Irenaeus, who was probably a teenager when Polycarp, at 86 years of age, was burned at the stake because he refused to renounce his faith in Christ.

On and on we could go, and probably in a single row across this auditorium, we could present an unbroken chain of people who passed down their faith until it reaches us today. Many of them, like Polycarp, sacrificed their very lives rather than renounce that faith. Truly we stand on the shoulders of giants, and we owe them a debt that we can only repay by building on what they accomplished, by sharing that faith with those around us, and passing it on to our children.

Although each of our stories is different, all of our lives are interwoven. Just as Jesus's disciples, while different in so many ways, all shared a common faith and dependence on their Lord, may that be said of us as well.

Whenever I speak about the Lord's Supper, I seem to keep coming back to the word "communion." We're united with our Lord, but we're also united with each other. When we take the Lord's Supper, it's hard to feel superior, because the very act itself reminds us that it is our sins that brought Jesus to this point. And it should make us feel that we're all in this together. We also recognize that the same has been true throughout the centuries, going back to that first time when the disciples took it with our Lord. We are united with them, just as surely as we are united with Christ and with one another, and that makes this experience rich indeed.

Giving What We Have

Until the American Civil War, the only paper currency the United States government had issued was during the Revolutionary War. After that, only gold and silver coins were issued by the government, while individual banks might issue paper currency, which is where we get the term "bank notes." But the cost of conducting the war made it difficult for the government to meet its obligations, and so, on February 25, 1862, Abraham Lincoln introduced the first United States paper currency, backed only by the good faith of the United States.

Lincoln once sat in a meeting in which his cabinet members were discussing what sort of motto to put on the new paper money. Some thought an appropriate motto would be "In God We Trust." Lincoln, expressing the dry humor for which he became famous, replied, "If you are going to put a legend on the greenbacks, I would suggest that of Peter and John: 'Silver and gold have I none; but such as I have give I thee.'"

I'm hesitant to speak for God, but it seems obvious to me that He is far more concerned that we give Him what we have than about the promises we might make about what we would give if we had more. There's a lot I don't understand about what God would have me do, but it's perhaps too easy to concentrate on that, instead of simply doing what I know He wants me to do.

And this is what God does. When He gives, it isn't a symbol or a vague promise. God gives the best in every circumstance. Nowhere do we see this principle more clearly demonstrated than in the death of Jesus. God didn't offer vague promises that we hope are true. Instead He offered His own Son, the most costly gift He could make. And He did it for us.

Jesus's death provides us with at least two lessons. First, it demonstrates how much God really loves us in terms that mere words could never express. But it also reminds us that God expects our response to be costly as well. It's a paradox that while salvation is free, God asks us to surrender everything to Him. He doesn't want just our gifts; He wants our very selves. Yes, we give only what we have, but we dare not offer less.

Communion Requires Community

I want you to think back for a moment about one special time from your childhood, especially a good time.

[Pause for a moment to give people time to think.]

While everyone here would have a different experience to relate, I feel fairly confident each situation would have one aspect in common. At least one other person was there to share the experience. While we can have significant and enjoyable times alone, it seems natural to cherish the experiences we can share with others.

Sometimes when we think about the Last Supper, we can become so focused on Jesus that we forget that the other disciples were also there. Jesus Himself told them how important they were. In Luke 22:15 He tells His disciples, "I have eagerly desired to eat this Passover with you before I suffer."

There's an old saying that goes something like this. "Shared experiences double the joy, but cut the pain in half." Take a moment to look around. We're about to share the Lord's Supper "together." We even call it "communion." But you can't commune by yourself. By definition, communion requires someone with whom to share the experience. A moment ago I asked you to look around. Look around again. Focus on certain special people. Perhaps it's a spouse sitting beside you, to whom you have committed your love and devotion and with whom you have shared so much joy, and, yes, a certain amount of sorrow too. Maybe it's a close friend, a golfing buddy, or someone who has watched the Super Bowl with you. Perhaps it's a loving woman who taught your children about God when they were just babies. You see, communion requires community. We can't share with people we don't know. Family should not be something we just call ourselves. It should be a word that truly describes what we mean to one other.

Jesus knew what was coming, and He wanted to share a special meal with those disciples who, despite their faults and limitations, had come to mean so much to Him. Now we too are going to participate in the Lord's Supper. Yes, we commune with God, but we also share it together, just as we have shared many of the important aspects of our lives.

Christ's Love Compels Us

Suggestion — I have written the first paragraph from my own perspective. You might wish to change it to reflect your background.

Did you ever hear anyone make the boast, "Nobody can make me do anything?" I'm inclined not to believe that. Plenty of people have been able to make me do all sorts of things I wouldn't have done without some prodding. When I was a child, making up my bed wasn't one of my favorite activities. We won't even talk about keeping my room clean. In high school and college I spent untold hours studying for tests and doing research for term papers, when I could think of many more pleasurable activities. Have you ever found yourself driving along the highway, and suddenly you see a patrol car on the side of the road? What did you do? If you're like me, you probably slowed down, even if you were already driving within the speed limit. A lot of people, most of them well-intentioned, have made me do things, and the reality is that I am a better person for the pressure they exerted.

But in 2 Corinthians 5, Paul talks about a different form of persuasion that had changed his life. He says in verse 14, "For Christ's love compels us." Now that's an entirely different form of influence, isn't it? Perhaps at no other time during the week do we feel that compulsion more fervently than when we participate in the Lord's Supper, because, as we take it, the love of Christ becomes so real.

So what does the love of Christ compel us to do? There are so many answers to that question, and the response may be somewhat different for each one of us. However, there are perhaps certain ways in which all of us should feel moved to respond to the love of Christ. The most obvious response, and perhaps the easiest, is simply to remember how much Jesus's love led Him to do for us. At the same time, His love should cause us to live our lives as He lived His, with that same sacrificial love that sees others' needs before our own. It should also become second nature to want to share that love with others who so desperately need it.

To a world that understood the burden of oppression, Jesus said, "For my yoke is easy and my burden is light." (Matthew 11:30). No, He did not come to replace one taskmaster with another, but His love compels us just the same.

It's All about Life

Suggestion — Read the first three paragraphs before the bread is passed.

The Last Supper appears to have occurred in the setting of the Jewish Passover, and the most recognizable symbol relating to the Passover is the sacrificial lamb. It's interesting then to consider that none of the accounts of the Last Supper contain any mention of the lamb, even though Jesus Himself is referred to as "our Passover lamb" (1 Corinthians 5:7). And would not a lamb have been a better symbol of His body? So it makes us wonder why we use bread instead of lamb. I can think of at least two possibilities.

One reason is imminently practical. Even today meat is expensive, and the cost of preparing a lamb each week could become a burden even in the United States. In other countries and certainly in the ancient world, meat is considered a luxury. Perhaps this is one more indication that God is not interested in making our lives difficult. He is more focused on our hearts. He always has been.

At the same time, bread, in its own way, is a universal symbol of life. Just because meat is expensive, it would have carried little meaning over the centuries for the vast majority of Christians who lived lives bordering on poverty. Bread, on the other hand, remains the one thing that stands between life and death for untold numbers of people. And so, it's appropriate to see Jesus's body symbolized in the bread, because, for millions of people today, as in the past, life itself is pictured most clearly in a crust of bread.

Suggestion — Wait and make these comments before the fruit of the vine is passed.

The Law of Moses clearly reveals the significance of blood. In Leviticus 17:11 we read, "For the life of a creature is in the blood, and I have given it to you to make atonement for yourselves on the altar; it is the blood that makes atonement for one's life." If you've ever received a blood transfusion or even given blood, you understand something of the significance blood holds for life. The fruit of the vine is perhaps an easier symbol to understand than the bread, but it's the reality behind that symbol that's important. In the Passover sacrifice, the blood of the lamb sprinkled on the altar symbolized the atoning sacrifice, which, by the death of the animal, took away sin. Jesus's willingness to shed His blood (and so forfeit His life) gave us so much more. Oh, His death did take away our sins, but it wasn't a one-time event, but rather the ability to remove every sin we have or ever will commit. Even more than that, His death provides us with new life, a life energized by the Holy Spirit, in which death is forever vanquished, and our eternity is assured by the continual cleansing of His blood. So you see, the Lord's Supper really is all about life.

We Are Never Called to the Small

How would you define success? For our world as a whole, success is often measured in two areas, the amount of possessions and wealth we accumulate, and the degree of power or prestige we achieve. By these standards, Jesus was a colossal failure. When He died, even the clothes He wore were taken from Him, and He had to be buried in a borrowed tomb. At the time, His death probably rated only a minor notation in Rome's official records. Not much upon which to build a legacy.

The reason for this disparity is that Jesus had a very different view of success. He knew what it would mean for Him, and although we may not like to think about it, He calls us to measure our own lives by the same definition.

Listen to what Jesus says in Luke 9:23-25. "[23]Then he said to them all: 'Whoever wants to be my disciple must deny themselves and take up their cross daily and follow me. [24]For whoever wants to save their life will lose it, but whoever loses their life for me will save it. [25]What good is it for someone to gain the whole world, and yet lose or forfeit their very self?'"

Have you ever considered just what your life is all about? As I get older, I find myself doing that far more than I did when I was young. Am I making a difference? When I'm gone, will my life have any impact on this world? Whether we phrase it that way or not, don't we all want our lives to mean something? The only legitimate question to consider is how can my life make a difference? Will wealth and power do it? Yes, in the short run those things may rate you a lengthy obituary, even a place in the history books. But is that enough? Is that all there is?

The problem with the world's definition of success is that it's too short-sided. Henry Drummond speaks eloquently of this when he reminds us that John says of the world, not that it is wrong, but that it passes away. We are called to a higher goal and a greater meaning for our lives. God never calls His people to the small. Rather, He challenges us to take a larger view, to dare to gaze into eternity as the measure of our lives. A story is told about the multi-billionaire Howard Hughes. It was said that at his funeral, one man whispered to his friend, "I wonder how much he left?" To which his friend replied, "All of it."

Jesus gave everything He had, even His life, for you and for me. And He calls us to do the same. He shows us the depth of His sacrifice, but only so we can imitate that in our own lives. So the Lord's Supper demonstrates both sacrifice as well as triumph, for one is necessary if we are to achieve the other. Today we remember Jesus's sacrifice — to acknowledge and appreciate it certainly, but also so that we may imitate it in our own lives.

The Most Significant Date in History

Does the date November 22, 1963, mean anything to you? Virtually everyone old enough remembers that date very well. Whether we remember it or not, I suspect that most of us immediately thought of the assassination of President John F. Kennedy which occurred on that date. But are you aware that another person died on that day, although President Kennedy's death ensured that it went virtually unnoticed?

You see, on that same date C. S. Lewis also died. I don't wish to take anything from President Kennedy, or diminish his influence. But a case could be made that C. S. Lewis may have been a force for good that matches or even exceeds that of John Kennedy. Consider the impact Lewis's writings have had on literally millions of people. How many Christians have had their faith grounded and supported by C. S. Lewis's brilliant ability to use reason and logic to explain difficult and even challenging concepts? How many non-believers, who perhaps simply assumed that a belief in Christ was not consistent with honest intellectual inquiry, were actually converted after reading how Lewis himself reached the conclusion that, from the standpoint of reason, there was no logical response but to accept the reality of the gospel message?

What the world sees as significant may not necessarily reflect reality, and I would suggest another date which is the real turning point in all of human history. Actually, it is not one date, but an approximately forty-hour period that covered portions of three days. I'm speaking of course about the death, burial, and resurrection of Jesus. What happened during this short period of time has had untold impact on human history. We can observe the effects even in our secular world. The teachings of Christ are incorporated into the legal codes of most countries of the western world. The very concept of hospitals, in the modern sense of the word, came from teaching about compassion for the sick. Poor houses and orphan homes can also be traced back to how Jesus said we should treat one another. And if you want to find the best marriage manual in the world, the one that really works if truly applied, just turn to the New Testament.

Of course, Christians believe that these few hours resulted in far more than that. If you're a Christian, then your assurance of eternity with God comes from what happened during these few hours. And that is their most lasting significance. The other results are good, and we should be grateful for how Jesus's teachings have changed our world for the better. But the most important result of Jesus's death, burial, and resurrection is what it provided for eternity.

The world as a whole may never recognize the significance of those three days in history, but let us never forget them, because our hope — indeed our assurance of eternal life — comes from those three short days.

Thanksgiving

Thanksgiving can be one of the more enjoyable holidays we celebrate, just because of its simplicity. There are no presents to buy or wrap. You don't have to keep up with the Joneses in terms of gifts, decorations, or anything else. For most of us, Thanksgiving revolves around eating too much, with perhaps less guilt than we would normally feel for doing so.

But for many of us, Thanksgiving is also about memories, perhaps some of the best memories we have from childhood. Many of us remember a time when we felt safe. The world seemed simpler, whether or not it actually was, and within the protection of our home, nothing could touch us. Oh, we understand now that wasn't the case. Hardship and tragedy are part of life, but back then we didn't know it yet. And every Thanksgiving, some of that feeling comes back. There's a place that provides a degree of security that we so desperately need in this chaotic and unpredictable world. And for that we can be thankful every year.

The Lord's Supper seems to offer some parallels to those feelings. There are no gifts, because we have nothing to offer. We don't compete with anyone else, because the Lord's Supper reminds us of our weakness and inadequacy.

We are often instructed to remember and be thankful for Jesus's sacrifice for us. That's okay, as far as it goes, but that approach seems to make thankfulness a duty. How can we produce gratitude on demand? No one ever had to tell me that it was my duty to get together with family every year, participate in a great meal, and be thankful for all that it represented. Just doing all that generates feelings of gratitude.

And so the Lord's Supper provides an opportunity once again for us to have security, to feel that there is truly nothing that can hurt us in an eternal sense. Yes, we recognize that we have problems today and may face tragedy tomorrow. None of that has gone away. But today we are reminded once again that, because of what the Lord's Supper represents, we have eternal security that no one can take away from us. I can't imagine not being thankful for that.

How Do You See Jesus?

In John 14:8 Philip asks Jesus to do something he must have thought was truly beyond the scope of reason. Philip says to Jesus, "Lord, show us the Father and that will be enough for us."

Let's not be too critical of Philip. Think about it for a moment. He had just asked to see God Himself, and he expressed enough faith in Jesus to believe it just might be possible for Jesus to grant his request. That seems like quite a lot of faith to me. In all honesty, I've never had the nerve to ask anything so bold in my own prayers.

So, what's the problem with Philip's request? It had already been answered. In fact, the answer was standing right before him, but he failed to see it. You see, he really didn't know Jesus quite as well as he thought he did. He understood enough about Jesus to believe that He possessed unbelievable power, but he failed to comprehend that Jesus was Himself the source of that power.

What about you? If you could ask anything you wanted, what request would you make of Jesus? Let's be honest now. Would it be something selfish — a Rolls-Royce, a luxury home, ten million dollars (or whatever the lottery is this week)? Perhaps your request would be nobler — an end to poverty, peace on earth, or maybe on a more personal level, the restoration of a relationship that had meant so much to you. What about the big one — eternal life? Surely that's what we need.

Oh, by the way, do you remember how Jesus

responded to Philip's request? "⁹Jesus answered: 'Don't you know me, Philip, even after I have been among you such a long time? Anyone who has seen me has seen the Father. How can you say, 'Show us the Father'?"

During the Last Supper, Jesus gave the disciples the answer to the question they should have been asking, although they would not understand it until three days later. What Jesus was telling them that night (and showing them the next day) was what all of us really need. It's not more or better stuff. It's not even restored relationships or world peace. What the world — what each one of us — needs is Jesus Himself. He didn't give us "something"; He gave us Himself. And He still does. Accept that, and all the rest will fall into place. Get everything else, but reject Jesus, and sooner or later we will recognize that we made a bad bargain. Jesus offered Himself one time in history, but He still offers Himself to each one of us — the best gift you will ever receive.

Walking With God

I suspect all of us have seen a marching band or a military parade. Have you ever considered what's involved in their keeping exactly together, even while they're all moving? The key is that every person must do exactly the same thing, in the same place, and at the same time. In the military, when the command "march" is given, each soldier immediately starts out with the left foot. The leader "counts cadence," which dictates when every step is to be taken. In this way, the entire unit moves as one.

What I've described sounds very similar to ritual. We've come to be suspicious of ritual, because it can so easily be misused. But ritual can have a positive impact, as it helps unite us in our common faith, ensuring that we're all moving in the same direction.

The danger comes when we think of our Christian walk exclusively in terms of ritual. The truth is that nothing we do in this building defines us as Christians. That occurs in the world. There are two important scriptures that talk about our walk, and in both our walk is primarily with God, not with one another.

The first is in the Old Testament. In Micah 6:8 we read, "He has shown you, O mortal, what is good. And what does the LORD require of you? To act justly and to love mercy and to walk humbly with your God." In the previous verses Israel had questioned why God was angry with them. In effect they said, "We do all the sacrifices and rituals. Does God want even more of them?" Micah's response is powerful and direct. He tells Israel that what

God truly desires is a way of living that demonstrates itself in justice and mercy and walking with God. Even in the Old Testament, it wasn't just about ritual.

1 John 1:7 uses a different image to describe the same message. "But if we walk in the light, as he is in the light, we have fellowship with one another, and the blood of Jesus, his Son, purifies us from all sin." Once again, what God wants is for us to walk with Him — not ahead, nor behind, but keeping in step with God.

What all this means is that our Christianity is to be defined, not by ritual, but by how we live our lives. During the Last Supper, Jesus washed the disciples' feet. Some groups use this as a basis for practicing foot washing in their services. While that might be acceptable as a symbol, I would disagree if we were to teach that this is to be the message we get from Jesus's example. Jesus used the image of washing the disciples' feet to teach a lesson. But the reality of that lesson was demonstrated the next day, when Jesus showed the real meaning by taking upon Himself the full burden of the cross.

As we participate in the Lord's Supper, if we view it only as a ritual, I doubt we will derive much from it. If that's all we see in it, it might be better not to take it. But if we really understand what we are doing, the Lord's Supper can be a powerful reminder of who we are and what Christ calls us to be, both as individuals and as a community.

Lazarus and Resurrection

Jesus spent most of His ministry in Galilee. Not only was this His home, but it was separated from the politics and intrigue of Jerusalem. For this reason Galilee provided Jesus a degree of safety. John tells us that it was the death of His friend Lazarus that provided the motivation for Jesus to return to Judea and ultimately be crucified.

In John 11:21 a grieving Martha berates Jesus for not coming sooner. "'Lord,' Martha said to Jesus, 'if you had been here, my brother would not have died.'" When Jesus attempts to comfort her with the promise, "[23]Your brother will rise again," Martha shows her ultimate faith, but also the reality of her grief when she replies, "[24]I know he will rise again in the resurrection at the last day." And it is to this statement that Jesus makes His bold promise, "[25]I am the resurrection and the life. The one who believes in me will live, even though they die; [26]and whoever lives by believing in me will never die."

Although Martha could not have appreciated it at the time, Jesus must have been experiencing some of the same feelings she was, because He knew that all too soon He was to go the way of Lazarus. But if Lazarus serves as a representation of Jesus's death, he also provides a foreshadowing of Jesus's resurrection. Even more than that, the raising of Lazarus provides a promise that all Jesus said was true. He was and is "the resurrection and the life."

Have you ever thought about what Lazarus's life was like from then on? The poet Robert Browning wrote a narrative poem in which an Arab doctor of the first century describes Lazarus after he had been raised. He is amazed at how Lazarus's priorities are changed. The doctor describes how Lazarus is totally unmoved even by armies that may be coming to attack his village, while a simple gesture from a child can have a powerful effect on him.

While certainly this poem is fiction, and we cannot know what Lazarus's life was like, it brings up an interesting question for us to consider. Has the knowledge that we have eternal life changed our priorities? Has it made us different from what we would be if Jesus had not died, if He had never been raised? Has the understanding that we are eternal beings caused us to see the world differently from those around us? Do we, like Martha, blindly believe in some sort of future life, or can we truly say we comprehend something of the magnitude of Jesus's promise, "I am the resurrection and the life"? And do our lives reflect our faith that Jesus has in fact, by His own death and resurrection, given us eternal life? Significant questions for us to consider as we take the Lord's Supper.

Ponderous Chains

Read Romans 7:21-24

In Charles Dickens's *A Christmas Carol*, the cold-hearted Ebenezer Scrooge is visited first by the ghost of his old partner, Jacob Marley. Scrooge is genuinely puzzled to discover that Marley is bound by a long heavy chain. When he inquires about it, Marley tells Scrooge that he too is bound by heavy chains, even though Scrooge cannot perceive them.

"Ponderous chains." Not a bad image to describe human beings. As Paul wrote in Romans 7, the central message of the gospel is that we are all weighed down by the heavy burden of sin. And, just like Scrooge in Dickens's story, we may have difficulty recognizing the powerful hold sin has on our lives. The image speaks to at least two kinds of people, and I suspect both are here today.

If you're not a Christian, you may not understand all this talk about sin. Perhaps you can honestly say, "I'm as good as the next person." Yes, and possibly no better than the next person either. The appropriate question has always been, "Am I good enough?" What about that ponderous burden of sin, so subtle that many of us aren't even aware of it? How is your family doing? The younger generation may laugh at *Ozzie and Harriet* and *Father Knows Best*. We replaced them with Archie Bunker and Bart Simpson. How about it? Has that worked out to be a good trade? Some of us are living with the reality of divorce or addiction — alcoholism, pornography, gambling or something else. And just like Scrooge, we pretend not to see it. But it's still there. Oh, yes it's there.

Perhaps you're a Christian. You know how to put on a good act, but deep inside there's emptiness, a loneliness that you seldom, if ever, let others see. Perhaps you too are afraid to recognize it, because possibly that makes you a hypocrite. Maybe, like Paul, you battle daily with that tug-of-war, tearing you apart inside, while outside you portray the righteous, smiling Christian image.

That's why the gospel is such good news. The gospel message is that Jesus took upon Himself that ponderous chain. We don't have to wear it any longer. And he wants to tear away that dysfunctional family, that unholy addiction that is slowly eating you from the inside out. That's what we commemorate in the Lord's Supper. It reminds us of Jesus's sacrifice for us, and in so doing, provides us with hope for tomorrow.

What about that chain you're wearing? Just for today, why not give it over to Him, and see if maybe you find that He's also willing to bear it tomorrow. That reality is what we celebrate today.

The Eye of a Hurricane

A hurricane can be one of the most destructive forces of nature. Some of you may have experienced the extremely high winds and torrential rains that are the most recognized features of a hurricane. Perhaps the strangest part of a hurricane occurs at its very center, what meteorologists refer to as the eye. As the hurricane passes over, the winds blow in one direction. Then, as the eye passes overhead, the winds and rains stop and the clouds break. If this happens during the day, the sun is visible; if at night, the stars shine overhead. There is absolute quiet and peacefulness inside the eye. Of course, that doesn't last. As the eye passes through, the force of the hurricane returns, with one difference. The winds are now blowing from the opposite direction.

Storms have often been used as a metaphor for the trials we experience in life, and we don't have to live very long before we encounter them in one form or another. It's true that some people undergo almost unimaginable trials, while others may appear to have a relatively easy life. While we will perhaps never be able to understand why, the reality is that no one is immune from suffering. In some form, it inevitably comes to all of us.

The same was true for Jesus. Even as a baby, life started out rough for Him, and He was, by any standard you wish to apply, always poor. Jesus's ministry shows us periods during which He was relatively popular, such as the feeding of the five thousand. At the same time, His teaching always seemed to bring Him into conflict with the religious leaders. For Jesus too, there were periods of calm, followed by times of conflict.

The Last Supper provided the last time of calm Jesus was to know during His earthly life, and I suspect He recognized that it was like the eye of a hurricane. The violence of the storm would come again very soon, more powerful and destructive than even He had experienced. We see it clearly in Gethsemane. Jesus knows what is about to happen. He can almost see it coming. But there is nothing He can do to avoid it.

That's part of what Hebrews 4:15 means when the writer tells us that Jesus was tempted just like we are. It doesn't just mean that He had the same kinds of temptation. He did, of course, but there is more to it than that. Jesus knew, as we do, that life is uncertain. It may be peaceful now, but struggle, trial, perhaps even failure, surely await us at some time and in some form. Part of the comfort we should take from this is the recognition that Jesus understands, because He experienced these struggles just as you and I do.

Are you in the calm now? Take a moment to recognize that it is His grace and His blessing that has brought you to this point. Maybe right now you're in the midst of a storm that seems ready to overwhelm you. But you see He knows what that's like too. Think for a moment. Is your trial any worse than His? And His promise to you is that eventually this storm, indeed all storms will pass, and we will finally experience the eternal peace that right now we cannot comprehend or begin to understand. He can promise that, because He experienced it.

Made in the USA
Las Vegas, NV
05 April 2024

88270145R00075